INNER SKIING
Is a Success . . .

"INNER SKIING is to other ski books as powder is to slush. After reading the book I experienced a spellbinding breakthrough in my freestyle skiing, as well as being better able to handle fear and concentration. Tim Gallwey and Bob Kriegel have created beautiful clear poetry of what skiing is really all about."

—Suzy Chaffee,
Olympic Skier,
three-time World
Freestyle Champion

INNER SKIING
Is Exhilarating

"The deeper you go into problems, the simpler they get. Learning to cope with the fear of skiing—or anything else—may be the most important outcome of applying the Inner Skiing technique."

—Minneapolis Star

INNER SKIING

"Timothy Gallwe̶
guru who gave th̶
OF TENNIS has t̶
Kriegel to produc̶
and you, too, can be graceful."

—Playboy

INNER SKIING

Timothy Gallwey and Bob Kriegel

BANTAM BOOKS
TORONTO/NEW YORK/LONDON

INNER SKIING

*A Bantam Book / published in association with
Random House, Inc.*

PRINTING HISTORY

*Random House edition published November 1977
7 printings through March 1979*

Playboy Book Club edition December 1977

Book of the Month Club edition June 1978

Sports Ilustrated Book Club edition June 1978

Serialized in Psychology Today *November 1977,* Creative Living *December 1977, the* Chicago Tribune *December 1977,* New Age Journal *January 1978 and* New Woman Magazine *April 1978.*

Bantam edition / November 1979

Grateful acknowledgment is made to the following for permission to reprint previously published material.

Macmillan Publishing Co., Inc., and Turnstone Press, Ltd., London: Excerpts from Jonathan Livingston Seagull *by Richard Bach. Copyright © 1970 by Richard D. Bach.*

California Living, The Magazine of the San Francisco Sunday Examiner & Chronicle: *Excerpts from the "California Living." Copyright © 1977 by California Living, the Magazine of the San Francisco Sunday Examiner & Chronicle.*

Cover photograph courtesy Focus on Sports.

ISBN 0–553–12162–6

Published simultaneously in the United States and Canada

Bantam Books are published by Bantam Books, Inc. Its trademark, consisting of the words "Bantam Books" and the portrayal of a bantam is Registered in U.S. Patent and Trademark Office and in other countries. Marca Registrada. Bantam Books, Inc., 666 Fifth Avenue, New York, New York 10019.

To Guru Maharaj Ji
with growing love
and devotion
TG

With great love
to the memory of my
father, Arthur Kriegel
BK

Desire is like a force. One force is generated by mind, and one is generated naturally within us, and just where these forces are directed determines how useful or harmful they are.

—Guru Maharaj Ji

Author's Note

The reader of a book written by two people deserves an explanation of how the authors combined their efforts. Though I realized that Inner Game principles had a practical contribution to make to skiing, my background in the sport was limited, and Bob Kriegel had not only the necessary experience in skiing and psychology, but also a practical understanding of the Inner Game. Consequently *Inner Skiing* is truly a collaborative effort; each of us shared in its conception and in the writing. Generally we would tape long discussions on the content and organization of each chapter, and from this Bob would then write a first draft. (For this reason the first person almost always refers to Bob.) I would write the second draft, and then we would polish this together.

It is altogether fitting that in writing this book we had to practice its precepts. Progress was only possible when each of us was able to let go of our Self 1 attachments to "mine," and to allow our Self 2 talents to cooperate creatively.

—T.G.

Contents

INNER SKIING

1
Skiing Is More than a Parallel Turn

Inner Skiing

There is a magic in skiing when all is going well which transcends anything I have experienced in other sports. As I soar down a mountainside letting my body find its own balance in turn after turn, my mind as clear as the cold air against my face, my heart feels as warm as the sun, and I attain a level of experience which compels me to return to the snow for more and more of the same.

But too often this magic turns to misery. Apprehensive thoughts intrude and I lose natural rhythm, repeat old mistakes, and fall needlessly. I pick myself up cold, wet and discouraged, wondering if skiing is worth the trouble after all. Will I ever get off the seemingly endless plateau in my progress and ski the way I'd like to? Will I ever soar again? Something tells me not to count on it, but another voice urges me to try.

The purpose of *Inner Skiing* is to increase the magic of skiing and decrease the misery—to bypass the frustrations which inhibit its joy and freedom, and to learn how to reach that state of mind in which we not only appreciate the sport but perform at our best. The premise of this approach is that primarily it is neither external conditions nor lack of technical expertise which prevents us

3

from experiencing skiing at its best, but the doubts, fears and thoughts within our own heads. The Inner Skier comes to recognize that his greatest challenge, and consequently his greatest possibilities, lie in overcoming the self-imposed mental limitations which prevent the full expression of his physical potential.

The fears and doubts in the mind are automatically transferred to the body in the form of tension, rigidity and awkwardness, preventing us not only from moving fluidly, but also from seeing the terrain clearly. Inner Skiing aims to develop the skills necessary to recognize and overcome these inner obstacles. Using this approach, the skier learns the art of relaxed concentration and to trust his body's potential to learn and perform. He discovers that the secret to success in skiing lies in not trying too hard, and that his best teacher is his own experience. He develops a true sense of self-confidence which allows him to view falls and mistakes as learning opportunities rather than reasons for anger and frustration.

The Inner Game approach is hardly new. It is similar to the natural way that, as children, we learn to walk, talk or throw a ball. It uses the unconscious, rather than the deliberately self-conscious, mind. This process doesn't have to be learned; we already know it. All that is needed is to unlearn the habits and concepts which interfere with our natural learning ability, and to trust the innate intelligence of our bodies.

The principles of the Inner Game approach to learning and to maximum performance are basically the same for most sports and other activities, but each sport presents its own unique inner and outer challenges. Tennis requires sustained visual concentration during long periods of physical exertion. Distance running offers special opportunities to overcome boredom and develop endurance. Golf demands the subtlest kind of mental concentration and kinesthetic control. Team sports teach us cooperation and how to sacrifice individual egos for the benefit of the team. The remainder of this chapter concerns the often-neglected opportunities offered by the special nature of skiing to learn some things more universally applicable than how to make a parallel turn. The parallel turn is not difficult once we rediscover *how* to learn.

Letting Go of What You Think You Know

Remember how strange and awkward it felt the first time you stepped into ski boots and strapped those long boards on to your feet? Remember how frightened and out of control you felt when you tried to move?

Most sports have one characteristic in common. Whether it is baseball, basketball, tennis, golf, hiking, climbing or boxing, the way we move on the earth is by walking or running. Even as beginners ignorant of the rudiments of these sports, we at least know how to move. But in skiing we must slide rather than walk or run, and so we relate to the ground and move on it in an entirely different way. When we first stand on a pair of skis we lose that feeling of having a firm foothold on solid ground. A slight shift of weight can cause us to lose our balance and fall.

Thus, in skiing we must confront a basic fear: *loss of the familiar.*

This feeling of uncertainty is similar to the first time we put our feet on the pedals of a bicycle, pushed off the wall of an ice-skating rink or tried to stay afloat in water. Just as in these other activities, learning to ski requires first being willing to let go of one known sense of control in order to gain another. In trying to do so, few of us escape a sense of panic. Learning to swim, we flail around in the water desperately trying to stay afloat. In skiing we hold our bodies rigid, hoping to prevent ourselves from falling. But our struggle to maintain control in a new medium usually interferes with more than it helps the effort to achieve that goal. Fighting the new element prevents us from adapting to it.

Our situation as a beginning skier is similar to being in a room when the lights go out. In pitchblackness our eyes—the primary means for gathering information about our world—are useless; we are literally in the dark. If we panic and grope blindly for the light, inevitably we will bump into objects and damage them or ourselves. On the other hand, if we allow our eyes to adjust to the dark, shapes will start to emerge and we will again feel secure. Similarly, in trying to ski, if we don't panic and fight the experience of sliding, our bodies soon grow accustomed to this new form of locomotion and we gain a sense of confidence.

Not having his basic references for moving his body, the frightened beginning skier tries to cling to his old and familiar ways. When trying to slow down or stop, his first reaction is to lean back and dig in his heels, just as he would when walking or running. In trying to prevent himself from falling down, he leans uphill. But in skiing, the laws of movement are different, and leaning back only makes you go faster, while leaning uphill causes the skis to slide out from under you. To the beginner, this reaction of his skis is as confusing as if he stepped on the brakes of his car, only to find it accelerating. He panics even more and leans back still further in a desperate attempt to stop, which causes him to increase speed, lose balance and fall.

I will always remember my first time on skis. I rode a rope tow to the top of a small hill, positioned myself in a basic snowplow as I had seen other beginners do, and pushed off. As soon as I began moving I became petrified at not knowing how to stop or slow down. My body, bent almost in half, was stiff with fear; I felt that if I relaxed one tightened muscle I would crash to the ground. In effect, I was a sliding statue. At first, whenever I began going too fast or reached the bottom, I would fall backwards, the only way I knew to stop. After a few runs, when I began to descend less slowly, the falls became more spectacular. Looking for a less painful way to stop, I tried unsuccessfully to stab my poles into the snow in front of me. My frustration only made me more determined to try still harder, biting my tongue and tensing my jaw. But the more I tried, the tighter I became and the more I fell.

Finally I said to myself, The hell with it. I'm going to stop fighting the hill and just ski. If I fall, I fall. I can't do any worse than I'm doing now. With this I felt a little more relaxed, and though it was scary to just let myself slide down, and though I still felt out of control, I didn't fall as frequently. After a few more runs, I started feeling my skis and noticing what happened when I leaned to one side or the other, or backward and forward. Gradually, by going with this new sliding motion, I began to gain a little control. Though I knew I wasn't turning properly, I was soon able to get where I wanted and to stop without falling. I was going to learn to ski after all!

Like anything else, learning to ski is a process of discovery which comes primarily from the experience itself. As we let go of our preconceived notions about how to move, we feel what it is like to slide on the snow. Without straining, our body learns from its experience, just as it did when learning to swim or ride a bike. By not resisting this new experience as we negotiate a slope we can learn far more than simply a new form of locomotion; we learn how to deal with the unexpected wherever we encounter it. We discover that we can adapt to strange or different experiences only when we are willing to let go of our dependence on old concepts.

A Chance to Overcome Fear

As he improves, the skier naturally wants to ski faster and take more difficult runs, to leave the slopes on which he is comfortable and try something new. But while taking his first chair to the top of the mountain or attempting a harder trail is exciting, it is also frightening.

Exceeding previous limits always involves risk and usually some fear, but it is the natural growth process which started when we first left the comfort and safety of the womb. The first time we attempt a more difficult slope, we take a chance on losing control; we may fall and get hurt or fail and be humiliated. Risk is like a pendulum: at one end of the swing is the excitement of growth and discovery; at the other end is fear.

Fear, which is probably the biggest obstacle to any learning process, is a repressive force. It exists in the mind, and almost always it is based on something that *might* happen in the future, rather than what *is* happening now. As Don Juan, the Yaqui Indian sorcerer, says, it is "the first of man's natural enemies . . . a terrible enemy, treacherous and difficult to overcome . . . If the man terrified in its presence runs away, his enemy will have put an end to his quest . . . he will never learn."

Learning to confront and overcome fear is one of the biggest challenges and opportunities in skiing. But it is not easy; in fact, it is often more difficult to overcome fear than to actually ski the slope itself. Yet as Don Juan says, "He must not run away, he must defy his fear . . . and take the next step in learning . . . and a moment will come when this enemy will retreat."

A skier may resist this challenge, saying, "I just want to learn to ski, not to overcome fear." But fear will slow his learning, and if and when he does improve despite remaining fearful, the skills he has mastered will be limited to the slopes. The Inner Skier chooses to confront and overcome fear. As a result, he improves not only his skiing, but also the quality of his life.

Cooperating with Nature

Watch an expert skier descend a trail; he flows like water in a mountain stream. He shifts weight to one side, then another, producing a series of smooth looping turns. By the slightest movement of his legs his direction changes. It seems so simple and natural; in contrast to the beginner's movements his seem effortless.

Skiing is similar to riding a bicycle downhill. Both acts require less physical and mental effort than we imagine. On a bike we need only sit, hold the handlebars and let the hill take us. As we pick up speed the bike responds to subtle movements of our hands with nearly no effort on our part. We lean slightly into each turn; balance is maintained without conscious thought, and the power is supplied by gravity. Skiing, too, can be effortless when we cooperate with gravity's forces instead of fighting them.

In most sports we rely on our own power to run or jump, throw a ball or swing a racket. But in skiing, gravity provides the power and pulls us down the slope. The only exertion necessary is to play with the pull—checking, turning, slowing and directing our movement.

Learning to play with this natural force is a useful experience in everyday living. From it we can learn to act in harmony with our changing surroundings, other people and ourselves. Relying on gravity clearly demonstrates the advantages of blending with and using existing forces to move toward a chosen goal.

During an off-mountain session of an Inner Skiing workshop I asked for two volunteers of about the same size. Keith, a young, bearded psychologist, and Arnie, a rugged-looking real estate entrepreneur in his forties, came forward. "Stand facing each other and hold your hands out shoulder height so that you are touching palms," I instructed. "Now the goal of this exercise is to get the other person off balance. You can move your hands any way you want. The only rule is that you can't move your feet, and that your hands must keep touching the other person's with the palms open. Okay, begin."

All became quiet as Keith and Arnie started moving their hands in big circles, giving a push here, a feint there. Then Arnie gave a hard shove forward, almost knocking Keith over backward. Recovering, Keith also started pushing in earnest. For the next few minutes the only sounds were the grunts of the two participants as they strained for an advantage. Suddenly it seemed as if Keith was winning. Using his superior strength, he was slowly pushing Arnie's arms backward. All looked lost for Arnie, until abruptly he relaxed his arms, causing Keith to lurch forward.

"Perfect," I said as everybody clapped and the two men sat down. "When Keith and Arnie tried to resist each other's strength, they used a lot of energy and tired quickly. But eventually Arnie won by blending with Keith's force and using it to his advantage. Blending, a basic principle in the martial arts, can also be used in skiing, teaching us when to flow with the force of gravity and when to resist it."

Later that morning I could feel fear in the air as a group of us stood at the top of a steep, moguled slope. "Maybe we should try another slope," Kerry said hesitantly. "This looks like crash city." A few others agreed.

"Let's try looking at the bumps in a different way," I suggested, trying to ease the tension. "Look at the slope as if it were an opponent in the 'push hands' game. Let's try to use the moguls to help us turn, instead of fighting against them the way most of us usually do."

The others in the group were hesitant, but Diane, who had been quite meek and silent all week, suddenly came alive. "We can even thank them for helping us," she said, giggling.

"Fine," said Keith. "Let's thank every mogul we use," and he started off.

Everybody followed, and it was comical to hear eight skiers going down this difficult slope yelling out "Thank you." Everyone seemed more relaxed and skied better, and those who fell didn't seem to mind. At the bottom, they all were laughing and wanted to do it again. Befriending our enemy had been fun and also had done much to improve our skiing.

Situation Skiing

Skiing is a sport of changes; no run is ever the same. Snow which was soft and smooth in the morning later in the day becomes rutted and packed down. Moguls increase in size as skiers keep pushing snow into them. The texture of the surface itself changes with shifts in temperature or exposure to the sun.

"Skiing is a sport of diversity, of differences," says Jean-Claude Killy, the Olympic triple gold medal winner. "To get more out of the mountain and from ourselves, it is important to learn to adjust to these different situations." In powder we sit back slightly on the tails of our skis, whereas if we did this on hardpack we would lose balance.

Many times I have skied a slope that I had taken only a few hours before. Thinking that I knew it well enough, I will take it for granted and let my mind wander, when suddenly I'll hit the unexpected—a patch of ice, a bare spot or a new mogul —and be thrown off balance, lose my rhythm, perhaps even fall. When you have preconceived notions about a slope, you won't truly experience it. You see the slope as you think it is, or as it was before, rather than as it is now. When you hit something, it comes as a surprise. This is the mountain's way of saying "Pay attention."

With an awareness that each run is different, we tend to concentrate more. Taking less for granted, we are more alert, our feeling for our skis and the snow increases, and our sensitivity to any changes in the terrain heightens. When the mind is in this state of alertness, the body is poised and ready to respond to any situation. Not only does our skiing improve, but we also have more fun.

The more we realize that nothing in this world ever stays the same, and that change is the only constant, the more acute our perceptions will be. We begin to see the world as it is, rather than through the screen of past concepts. The present seems alive and fresh, and we are more able to respond appropriately to the novelty and difference inherent in each moment.

Slowing Down to See

When I lived in New York City, I remember longing to spend a few days in the country away from the cement, fumes and frantic rush. I'd dream about walking through the woods, feeling the earth under my feet, seeing the sky overhead. Then I'd get away for a weekend and be in such a hurry I'd never even notice where I was.

What was I doing on these trips? Frantic skiing, of course. My friends and I would leave the city on Friday evening, drive for five hours and arrive exhausted. Nevertheless, we'd awaken at dawn, gulp down breakfast and rush to the mountain, where we'd ski all day, not stopping even for lunch. The only chance we had to relax was in the lift lines, but of course we were tense there as well, moaning about how slow the lines were moving. Whenever the chair stopped, the delay was like death.

For all the nature I took in on those weekends, I might as well have been skiing in the Manhattan subway. Sure, I'd be looking out at my surroundings, but mostly to gauge how long the lift line was going to be, or on which slope the snow was best.

Then one Saturday I was coming alone down a big bowl, only to find, after thirty yards, that it was crusty and unskiable. I was too far down to return to the top, so I had to cross over and hike uphill to reach an adjoining slope. I was really annoyed; precious skiing time was being wasted. When I reached the top of the slope, I was out of breath and stopped to rest. At this moment the light on a patch of snow caught my eye. It looked as if the snow was bursting with all the colors of the spectrum. Suddenly it occurred to me that in all my years of skiing in some of the most beautiful places in the world, I had never really opened my eyes. I looked around, seeing as if for the first time the colors of the trees, the snow, the sky and the shapes of the mountains on the horizon.

That evening, still moved by this encounter with nature, I decided to stay in our lodge rather than go partying with my friends. Watching the fire dance in the hearth, I realized that the way I had been skiing was a reflection of my life. Everything was done in a rush; I worked, came home, changed clothes and went out again. I thought I had to move fast or I'd be left behind.

Seeing that light reflecting off the snow changed my approach and attitude not just to skiing, but to life in general. Today I would rather take my time feeling the exhilaration of my body in motion, and observing the beauty of my surroundings, than rush down the mountain in order to get in a few more runs. I also see the futility of thinking that more is necessarily better, whether in ski runs or possessions. I have begun to pay more attention to the quality of what I am doing rather than to the quantity.

To Win Is to Enjoy

When we participate in a sport in which the object is winning or reaching a destination point, we tend to think about the score, the goal, the end of the journey. Our efforts are concentrated on what we must do to beat our opponent, and if we aren't winning, we aren't enjoying. But the pleasures of skiing lie in being totally involved, in the way we feel when the body is in motion—the delight in a turn skillfully executed, the sense of our own natural rhythm and flow. The goal is a feeling of harmony both with ourselves and with our environment. The prize is in the process itself. Hence, skiing can teach us something that is often overlooked in our goal-oriented daily activities: *the importance of enjoying the process.* From it we can learn that without appreciating the path, reaching the goal is often meaningless. Moreover, we discover that games of all kinds are more often won when first they are enjoyed.

So there is more to skiing than learning parallel turns. For the skier who recognizes the further possibilities his sport offers for learning how to learn, for overcoming fears and self-doubt, for gaining concentration and appreciation for nature, skiing becomes *re-creation* in the original sense of the word: an opportunity to discover something important about oneself and to learn skills that improve not only one's skiing but the quality of one's life.

2

Breakthrough and Breakdown:
Self 1 and Self 2

Breakthrough Runs

All of us have had those incredible runs when for
some reason everything seems to click and we ski
so much better than usual that we surprise ourselves. Turns we've been struggling with are suddenly easy. Frustrations vanish and we become
totally absorbed in the joy of the moment. The
usual mental struggle—trying to do everything
right, worrying about how we look or about falling
and failing—is forgotten. Enjoyment is so intense
that we don't even think of making a mistake—
and we don't. The thinking mind is in a state of
rest; awareness is at a peak. For a time, self-imposed limitations are forgotten; we are skiing unconsciously.

Runs like these make us forget tight boots, cold
hands, long lift lines and the eternal dissatisfac-
tion of not skiing as well as we want to. It is the
memory of these magical moments which draws us
back to the slopes time and again in hopes of
recapturing them.

Jan, a twenty-two-year-old college student who
had told me that she thought she was too uncoordinated to learn to ski, had just such an experience the fourth day she was on skis.

"It was the first time I took a run and really felt

in control," she said. "Up to that point, I was always hesitant, holding back and scared to death. I usually felt so awkward that I didn't believe I could ever learn to make a proper turn. But all my doubts left me on that run. For the first time I felt loose and relaxed, and for some reason it was easy to stop and turn whenever I wanted. I couldn't believe it; I wasn't even afraid of falling. After that one run I felt like a skier!"

"How did that happen?" I asked.

"That's the funny thing, I can't tell you what I did—in fact, I don't think I *did* anything! It just seemed to happen, and I went with it. I felt so free and light!" Jan was obviously still enraptured by the memory of that moment.

One day last year I had a similar experience. I had skied hard all day, but not very well. This was to be my last run, and I resolved to take it easy on a slope that was challenging but not too difficult. But instead of pushing off right away as I usually did, I stood at the top of the run for a moment, taking in the silence of the world around me. Then, as I started down and took a few turns, I knew that something was different. I felt as if I were gliding effortlessly. Instead of planning where to turn, I seemed to know instinctively. I didn't have to think at all; it was as if the mountain was showing me the way. Moguls, usually my enemies, now seemed like old friends. I was turning on them and jumping off them as if I had been doing it all my life. It was more like flying down the mountain! I couldn't believe that I could ski like this.

Halfway down the trail I noticed another skier ahead of me, and I fell in about twenty yards behind him, following his tracks. The two of us floated down the mountain in unison in a silent dance. By the time we reached the bottom I was glowing, and I coasted over to the other skier, whose grin was even bigger than mine. The expression on his face was matched by the exhiliration in his voice as he said, "It was a breakthrough run—my God, I never thought I could ski like that."

Toasting our great run at the bar, my new friend, a surgeon from New York, tried to analyze how without really trying he had skied far better than he ever had before. "You know," he told me, "sometimes I get that same feeling when I'm doing surgery—that sense of total involvement with a greater kind of knowing, and along with it an incredible dexterity and alertness."

This breakthrough experience is one we've all had at different times in our lives. It is the feeling of "getting hot" in a basketball game, of playing "out of your head" in a tennis match, of losing yourself while jogging or swimming. It is the feeling of dancing to music when it seems to be emanating from inside your body. But breakthroughs are not limited to physical activities; they can occur at any time and in any activity. They are those creative flashes when the solution to a problem emerges at the instant you least expect it, the intuitive eureka.

However, much to our chagrin, breakthroughs in skiing or in any other activity virtually never happen when we plan them, and therefore they usually seem accidental. But they don't happen by chance. On the mountain they occur when we are so engrossed that we are no longer thinking about the next turn or judging the last one. In fact, breakthroughs appear *only when we stop thinking.*

This nonthinking, spontaneous state in which we

let ourselves float in the experience of the moment is what we call "skiing out of your mind." But like being in love, as soon as we start thinking about how to keep ourselves in this ecstatic state, we lose it. Methodically we then set out to regain our lost sense of mastery by working on our technique, item by item. But the thrill is gone; we are back in the mind.

These breakthrough runs, which skiers at all levels experience, have a special significance; they help us to recognize our inherent possibilities. Without them a skier might reasonably conclude that he or she is *innately* awkward or uncoordinated. But the breakthrough confronts us with an undeniable and somewhat uncomfortable truth: we *can* perform much better than we usually do. In light of this realization, our usual excuses—we haven't skied enough recently, haven't had enough lessons, or are just plain uncoordinated—crumble. We can only conclude that the reason we don't normally perform so well is not that we don't have the ability, but that we somehow interfere with it. In the breakthrough run we skied beyond our expectations not because we finally mastered a new technique but because for a few moments our state of mind changed. The mind became quiet, making our movements more natural and coordinated. Such occasions indicate that the excellence of our skiing is dependent more on our state of mind than on the selfconscious mastery of memorized techniques.

To suppress the uncomfortable fact that it is we ourselves who interfere with our ability to ski up to our demonstrated potential, we often prefer to attribute breakthroughs to luck, good snow conditions, newly sharpened edges or, most commonly, to a tip from another skier. But at some level we understand that in spite of its infrequent occurrence, skiing "out of one's mind" is as natural as running or laughing, that it is a true expression of how skiing could be more often.

I spend a lot of time with someone who has these experiences much more frequently than I do. His name is Otis. He is supple and loose, moving naturally and easily, reacting spontaneously to whatever the situation demands of him on or off the mountain. His fun-loving attitude is contagious. Without pushing himself or ever trying too hard, Otis is constantly exploring, testing and going beyond his limits. He seems to have an inexhaustible supply of energy, and complete trust in his body. He is a natural athlete, but not at all an uncommon one for his age. He is my son and he is four years old.

After a year of volunteer supervision at Otis's nursery school, I still observe with wonder the joy, excitement and natural ease of children as they run, jump, climb and ride their tricycles. I have learned from them how easily and effortlessly we can move when we trust our bodies to do what they know best. At Otis's age we were all natural athletes; each of us had that sense of ease and excitement as we rejoiced in the movement of our bodies. The games lasted past dark, ending only with a parent's repeated yells to come in for dinner. There were endless days of excitement, of laughing and crying, of dirty knees, ripped shirts and scraped elbows. It was a time when everybody played unselfconsciously, a time so filled with breakthrough moments that we were oblivious to them.

Carrie Bachelder, an instructor in our Inner Skiing clinic, told me about playing a children's game with her class. "I was the hare and they were all hounds chasing after me, yelling and growling, trying to catch me. They totally forgot all about dos and don'ts. At the bottom of the run, Terry, a college professor, said, 'I felt like a kid again. I was so intent on catching the hare that I forgot all about my skiing, and, you know, I think I skied better than I have all week. I haven't had fun like that in years.' The other 'hounds' reported similar improvement."

In their preoccupation with the chase, Terry and the others were allowing themselves to ski without thinking. As a result, they recaptured the spontaneous quality of physical play they had known as children, and rediscovered a state of mind conducive to peak performance.

Breakthrough to Breakdown

The morning after our breakthrough run, I met my friend the surgeon again. In fact, we almost crashed into each other; he was careening off a mogul, limbs flying in all directions. After what seemed like an eternity in this position, he fell and passed me in a slide that would have made the late Jackie Robinson envious. Muttering to himself through clenched teeth, he got up slowly, beating the snow with his ski pole as if it were to blame for his crash landing.

Gradually Doc calmed down and we took a few runs together. But he certainly was skiing less well than he had the day before. His movements, which had been so natural and easy, were now stiff and forced, and he was hesitant and visibly frustrated. If the day before had produced a breakthrough, today was a breakdown.

Later, back at the lodge, Doc said "I just don't understand how on one run I can do everything right, and then fall apart on the next."

Then in the next breath Doc proceeded to explain exactly why this happened. That morning he had been so eager to try to repeat yesterday's experience that as he started down he began giving himself helpful suggestions: "Remember, keep your weight forward . . . Edge a little more . . . Don't forget to step onto your uphill ski early in the turn . . ." But the more he coached himself, the worse he skied. As a result, he started to get angry, and to criticize himself for his mistakes: "You're leaning too far back, you jerk. Bend your knees more." The harder he tried, the more forced and strained his skiing became. The magic was gone.

Being at the peak of one's power is an incredible feeling. When it is gone, we naturally want to get it back again, but usually our very efforts to regain it only drive it further away, leaving us frustrated. Deliberate attempts to re-create effortlessness and spontaneity only achieve the opposite, raising the question: How can one attain results without trying?

Breakthrough experiences don't occur by trying to make them happen. That's not how our first such experience happened, nor how our next will. Trying to have a breakthrough experience is like trying to grab a wisp of smoke; not only can you not do it, but you will only become frustrated if you persist in the attempt. Time and again experience shows us that the part of us that tries is the *obstacle* to our true potential. It is a truly different part of us that skis our best and makes a natural effort without straining. You can increase the frequency of your breakthrough experiences if you understand more about these two parts of yourself.

Self 1 and Self 2

Listen to the thoughts that stream through your mind as you ski. Most minds are active with a flow of instructions about how to do this and how to avoid doing *that*—self-criticism, self-analysis, worries, fears and doubts. In many cases the chatter is continuous and often less than friendly. Step back for a moment and attend to these voices. Who is instructing, criticizing, and doubting whom? A person might answer, "I'm just talking to myself." Fine, but who is the "I" and who is the "myself"? Clearly they have different identities, or else they wouldn't be conversing. There would be no need for a conversation if there was only one party, because the one speaking would already know what was going to be said and so have no need to say it. That's why when we're at one with ourselves there is no internal dialogue and we experience inner peace.

In following the Inner Game approach, recall that the voice doing all the talking, judging, worrying and doubting is Self 1, and that it is instructing Self 2, the body that performs the actions. Self 1 is the ego mind that has to be in control, so it tells you how or how not to ski, that you are hopeless or great, that you are better than Joe, but not as good as Jim, and so forth. In most minds, these two selves don't get along well, a condition that makes skiing one's best impossible. In fact, if Self 1 and Self 2 were actually two separate persons, their relationship would be so clearly perceived to be based on mistrust that no one would even suggest that they try to cooperate.

Although Self 1 may sound as if it is the expert in skiing and everything else, through experience we soon discover that we perform best when we are thinking least. During breakthrough runs Self 1 is in a rare state of quiet. Control shifts to the nonverbal innate guidance system within our bodies, and our actions are directed silently. Self 1 is sometimes embarrassed and humbled by the recognition that we ski best when we are "out of our minds," but more often it resists admitting that over-conceptualizing—indeed, any conscious thought at all—interferes with the expression of our highest capabilities.

Once we understand that it is the mind—Self 1 —and its collection of self-concepts, doubts and fears accumulated over a lifetime which cause breakdowns and prevent optimal skiing, we can stop blaming our equipment, other people, snow conditions, and moguls. When Self 1 is in a quiet state, our awareness increases and we discover Self 2, that part of us that can respond to any situation instantaneously with its fullest capabilities. Self 2, our innate potential, already exists within each of us; we catch a glimpse of it every time we experience a breakthrough. Hence, the main objective of the Inner Game is to free ourselves of whatever inner obstacles prevent Self 2's fullest expression and development.

Who Is Self 2?

Although it isn't easy to conceptualize the difference between Self 1 and Self 2, it isn't difficult to detect the difference in skiing performed under these two influences. When we asked an Inner Skiing clinic at Copper Mountain to come up with words which describe skiing under Self 1's control in contrast with Self 2's the following words were used:

Self 1	Self 2
Trying	Free
Tense	Exhilarated
Mechanical	Light
Bored	Flowing
Unsure	Smooth
Scared	Relaxed
Distracted	Effortless
Struggling	Gravity
Thinking	Powerful
Expectations	Quiet
Angry	Speed
Heavy	Surprise
Hesitant	Soft
Choppy	Magical
Preconceiving	Flying
Holding Back	Rhythmic
Confused	Floating
Oh, my God!	Ecstatic

Think of all the actions that must be performed simply to turn your skis: shifting weight to the outside leg, bending the knee and ankle forward and laterally to increase edge control, moving your shoulder, arm and hand to plant your pole, shifting your weight by stepping onto the uphill ski—and countless other movements too numerous and subtle to describe. Any movement we make in skiing —or in anything else, for that matter—requires literally hundreds of instantaneous instructions from the nervous system to different muscle groups in our bodies.

Who is doing all this? Whoever, it is certainly a lot more sophisticated and competent than a nagging Self 1 who, thinking it is in control, keeps yelling, "Bend your knees, stupid!" Just who is being stupid?

Self 2 is the name we give to the total potential that exists within each of us. In his book *On Physical Education* the Indian scholar Sri Aurobindo described what we call Self 2 as "the essential and instinctive body consciousness which can see and do what is necessary without any mental thought . . . it is equivalent in the body to swift insight in the mind and spontaneous and rapid decision in the will." But there is nothing innately spiritual or mystical about Self 2 which makes it magically appear at certain moments. It is always within us, and it expresses itself to the extent that we can ignore the interference of the mind, Self 1. Self 2 is the basic intelligence which includes the central nervous system, the brain and other parts of our sensory apparatus we don't even know about. Whatever we do—each movement we make, each word we speak—is too complex an operation to be controlled by our conscious mind.

Self 1 could never learn the multitude of instructions necessary for even the simplest such task, much less communicate them instantaneously to our muscles. Therefore Self 2 expresses itself not just during breakthrough runs, but also in the most mundane activities: washing dishes, hammering a nail, getting dressed, eating. The complexities involved are truly amazing. Consider the act of hammering a nail. Initially you must exert pressure with the fingers of one hand to position the nail in place, then grip the hammer with the fingers of your other hand, flexing the forearm enough to keep the grip firm but not so hard as to lose flexibility. Next you must tighten the biceps to bend your elbow and rotate your shoulder to raise your arm while cocking your wrist at the top of the swing. All this and more just in order to get the hammer in position before bringing it down on the head of the nail! Then comes the amazingly complex hand-eye coordination which guides the hammer to the nailhead. Self 1 could never learn by itself to do the least complicated of these actions.

The fullest expression of Self 2 usually occurs during early childhood, before we accumulate limiting and distorted self-concepts. The child learns and performs with a minimum amount of Self 1 interference, which is why his movements look so natural, no matter what his level of proficiency. If a child started "trying too hard," criticizing himself for his lack of progress and thinking about how he moved, we would think it very unnatural. It would be—and it is just as unnatural when we do it as adults. It seems normal only because we've done it for so long that we've grown accustomed to it.

Who Is Self 1?

You can find the answer to this question by taking a moment to listen to the almost interminable stream of thoughts inside your head. On the mountain Self 1 may be squawking some of the following:

"Bend your knees."

"Keep your weight on your downhill ski."

"That was a lousy turn. You didn't edge enough."

"You'll never learn."

"You're too uncoordinated for this sport."

"You'll never be any good."

"This slope is too steep for you."

"Look at those moguls! You'll wipe out for sure."

"Don't be a chicken. If those turkeys can do it so can you."

"Keep your skis together and try to look good under the chair lift."

Obviously Self 1 thinks it knows all the answers because it is always telling you how to ski, evaluating and judging your progress, criticizing your mistakes, doubting your ability and comparing it with others', warning and worrying about failing and falling. In sum, Self 1 is an extremely complex character who plays a lot of different roles. Some of these are:

THE INSTRUCTOR He is constantly telling you everything you should be doing, how you should do it and when. "Keep your weight on your downhill ski . . . No, not that much, you'll lose your balance . . . Now shift your weight to the inside edge of your outside ski and roll your ankles across the fall line . . ." Afraid that nothing will go right if he's not talking, the Instructor loves to repeat his dictum: "Bend your knees, bendyourknees, bendyurnees!" Not only is he convinced that you can't learn to ski without him, but he also assumes that you have a very short memory! If I had to pay for all the instructions my Self 1 gives me, I couldn't afford the price of a lift ticket.

HELPLESS HARRY The opposite of the Instructor, Helpless doesn't trust you to be able to do anything for yourself. He always foresees problems, and wants to ask for help, advice or information, whether you need it or not. Instead of urging you to get up when you fall, and to put your own ski back on, he advises you to lie in the snow until somebody stops. If you follow Helpless's advice, you become overly dependent on others, and are usually the last to get your skis on and the last one down the slope. Like Laurel and Hardy, Helpless and the Instructor make a great pair: one thinks he knows everything and is constantly giving instructions; the other thinks he knows nothing and is constantly seeking them.

FLASHY FRED is not as concerned with how well you ski as with how well you look. Continually worried about what others think of you, he cripples you through self-consciousness and urges you to impress onlookers with your flashiest form. His ultimate high is to have you ski under the lift so that everyone can see you—provided, of course, that the trail isn't too difficult. But without spectators to applaud you, Flashy Fred has all the motivation of a leaky balloon.

THE COMPETITOR is always comparing your

skiing with someone else's, urging you to try to ski faster and further than those around you. He also wants you to know the fastest route to the mountain and how to get the best deal on equipment. Jaw tightened in determination; he feels betrayed if you ever want simply to relax and enjoy yourself.

FEARFUL is obsessed with falling and failing, and is afraid of bruising both your body and your ego. His favorite phrase is "Uh-oh, here comes ..." His second favorite is "I can't ski this!" His tension as he searches for signs of disaster is contagious, spreading tightness throughout your body, making you look as wooden as a cigar-store Indian on skis.

FEARLESS is bored skiing a slope within your competence. He loves risk and hates speeds that are under control. For him the perfect run is to flirt with disaster from the top of the mountain to the bottom. As he makes you fly down expert slopes looking as if you're going to crash and burn at any moment, his recklessness imperils not only yourself but almost everyone else.

THE KLUTZ is convinced that when God was handing out coordination, you dropped it. He knows beforehand that you will fail at anything athletic, and just to make sure that this occurs he constantly tells you what an awkward, slow learner you are. He also feels it important to tell everyone else how uncoordinated you are, just in case someone expects you to be able to ski. What frightens Klutz most is your having a good run when someone is looking; it destroys the self-image he has set up for you.

THE CRITIC has something negative to say about everything you do. Even if your turn is 99 percent perfect, he'll focus on the 1 percent error. His high standards aren't as annoying as his refusal to admit your current ability. He doesn't want you to become expert because it would put him out of a job.

Perhaps in the above you've recognized some of your own Self 1 roles. Here are a few others: Julius Judge, Horatio Hero, Nervous Nellie, Top Sergeant, Ego Tripper, Harriet Helper.

One word of caution. We can become so involved with the task of identifying and analyzing various Self 1 disguises that we neglect our skiing. This is simply one more of Self 1's roles—the Analyst. He gets us thinking so much about the cause of a bad turn or fall, or even how to cope with another Self 1 persona, that we lose touch with the present experience.

Self 1 would have us believe that he is indispensable to skiing and life, but in fact his constant chatter interferes with performance. This becomes apparent when we remember how quiet and thoughtfree the mind is when we are performing at our best. During a breakthrough run the mind is not directing, criticizing, judging, analyzing or being fearful; instead, it is quietly focused on the present.

One Self 1 role which frequently emerges to sabotage my own skiing is Flashy Fred, who wants me to impress onlookers. Typically he takes over when I am skiing under the chair lift. At the beginning of a run I am paying attention only to my skiing; then suddenly I become aware of the people overhead riding the lift. Foolishly I imagine that they are all looking at me, and my concentration switches from my skiing to them. But when I'm onstage, with the lift riders as my audience, I usually don't ski as well, and often attract their attention only with a spectacular crash.

Self 1's demands on our attention rob us of the energy needed to see the slope clearly or to feel movement and our skis. It is because of this limited awareness that we make mistakes, lose control and fall more often. The worse we ski, the more we strain, and this in turn causes tightness and awkwardness, resulting in further loss of balance and control. "See," Self 1 then shouts triumphantly. "You're not good enough for this slope." Thus the mental stress translates directly into physical movements.

This connection between thought and action has been described well by Dr. Roberto Assagioli in *The Act of Will:* "Images, mental pictures and ideas tend to produce the physical conditions and the external acts that correspond to them."

Self 1's basic goal is to ensure its own survival and continuing influence over your skiing and your life. To this end it will even go so far as to pretend to undertake the project of getting rid of itself. After reading this chapter, for instance, you may grow impatient with your foibles and shortcomings, frustrated at not allowing Self 2 to be in charge more often, and hence chastise yourself whenever Self 1 is in control. But instead of judging your skiing, now you are judging yourself for being judgmental and for not playing the Inner Game well! Instead of straining to ski well, you now strain to be in the present moment and try hard to not try hard! Thus Self 1 is perpetuated and retains control indefinitely. We call this Self 1 persona the New Age Judge. He tells us how we should *be* rather than how we should *ski*. Sly, isn't he? He has an inexhaustible set of disguises, so dealing with him requires that first we must be able to recognize him before we can tame him.

Taming Self 1

Self 1 is stronger than we think, and not easy to silence. Its different roles are like wild horses which we let pull us in many directions all day long. Then when we decide to use them for a single goal we grow frustrated because they won't pull in unison and respond to our commands. We all would like our minds to stay quietly in the present when we ski, but can we keep it from worrying about the next turn or criticizing the one we just made? Few believe that their fears and self-doubts are really helpful, but can we silence them? To what extent do we control the reins of our own thoughts?

If we try to fight Self 1 head-on, we find ourselves in a battle that we can't possibly win. We create an interminable civil war in our heads which is diametrically opposite to the state of peace we are seeking. Ultimately, the mind is controlled not by fighting with it but by taming it, by gradually regaining our rightful authority over our own thoughts, so that instead of letting them take us where they want to go, we set the direction. The entire process of the Inner Game described in these pages is directed toward the simple goal of quieting the mind so that Self 2 is free to express its true abilities and chosen direction.

The process of regaining your mastery over Self

1 starts with the simple recognition of its existence. Yet we must also realize that Self 1 is not who we really are. When we observe the thoughts and roles of the mind, we know that we and the thoughts are different. By observing Self 1 nonjudgmentally, we no longer identify with it; we simply watch it. As soon as I see Flashy Fred for who he is, I can separate myself from him and can choose to refocus my attention on my skiing. Separating from Self 1 is like being aware that a dream, while it is still going on, is only a dream; as a result, the illusion no longer has the same power or control over us. Similarly, the degree to which we can step back from Self 1 and no longer be subject to its doubts, fears and desires is the measure of our success in taming him. As we approach this goal, Self 2 will become more apparent and will have an easier time expressing itself.

Trusting Self 2

The Inner Game approach to releasing our potential involves two basic steps: quieting Self 1 and trusting Self 2—which is to say, quieting the mind and trusting the body. These two skills go hand in hand, and each is necessary in order to achieve success. The reason Self 1 is so active is that it doesn't trust the abilities of the body. Else, why all those repeated instructions? Trusting Self 2 means allowing it to control the actions of the body. This doesn't mean that if a beginning skier trusts his body he will immediately ski like an expert; what it does mean is letting the body do what it already can and trusting that it will learn how to do what it can't yet do.

Why should we trust Self 2? Simply because it is more trustworthy than Self 1 in terms of both performance and ability to learn, as all of us have discovered on breakthrough runs. Another word for trusting Self 2 is confidence, which is nothing more than Self 1's recognition of the amazing abilities of Self 2. It is commonly recognized that confidence is essential to high-level performance, but not so commonly understood is how we come by this elusive quality. Trusting our own potential is at once an act of the will and a process. Consider the example of a father teaching his fifteen-year-old son to drive a car. Intellectually he may decide to trust his son, but confidence in him will develop only when, over a period of time, the son's driving skills give evidence that the trust is well placed. At first the father may trust his son to drive only in an empty parking lot, and then on a country road. Certainly he doesn't give the boy the keys and let him loose on the freeway, any more than a responsible ski instructor will lead a beginner down an advanced run. Trust is important, but it should be given to the individual skier according to his ability and the situation. If the father teaching his son to drive is constantly barking instructions to him, and even grabs the wheel himself whenever another car comes in sight, little learning will take place and there is little chance for confidence to grow. Similarly, when we don't trust ourselves to learn from experience, we seriously hamper our development.

We will never learn whether or not Self 2 is reliable unless we allow it to take control, and if we allow Self 1 to reassert itself every time we make a mistake, we will never discover Self 2's ability to correct itself. Regaining confidence in Self 2 takes time, but the process can't even begin unless we *decide* to trust it and give it a chance to show what it can do. Whenever we are doubtful of Self 2's ability to learn to ski, we can ask ourselves to remember how we instinctively corrected ourselves after our falls when we were learning to walk at about the age of a year.

The remainder of this book is about how to increase our ability to quiet the interferences of the mind and to develop a recognition of, and trust in, our innate abilities to perform and learn.

3
Natural Learning
Is Sense-able

Kids Learn Easier

Dick, a close friend, recently came to visit me. He hadn't been on the slopes for a few years and had decided to take his children on a week-long skiing trip. Eager to teach his youngest son, Ben, who was six years old, he asked, "How do you go about teaching someone that age?"

"The most important thing to remember is not to try to teach him too much," I answered. "Make sure he's warm and comfortable and, above all, let him have fun. The rest will take care of itself. Don't give him too many instructions—in fact, the fewer the better." I also told him about a few games he could play with Ben as they skied together.

A few weeks later Dick dropped by again, and I asked him about the trip. "You should have seen Ben," he said. "He's a natural! He just bombed down the beginners' slope the first day as if he'd been doing it his whole life. He was even turning pretty well, without more than a hint from me. He fell once in a while but it didn't bother him at all —he'd just get up and go at it again.

"I felt pretty rusty," Dick continued, "so one morning I decided to take a lesson. My instructor was a really hot skier and seemed to be a good teacher, but I guess I wasn't that good a student. I really had a hard time. I tried to remember his instructions, and if I'd been able to get my body to do what I was telling it, I'd have been in good shape. As it was, I found it frustrating. No matter what I did, I couldn't seem to regain my old form. Later, when I saw Ben skiing so effortlessly I got a headache—I was having so much trouble doing something that supposedly I already knew how to do and there he was, skiing so easily his first time out. Though he hadn't acquired any refinements yet, there was a naturalness to his skiing that I envied—plus the fact that he was enjoying himself so much."

The main difference between Ben's and Dick's learning experience was their states of mind. Dick was continually thinking about how to ski, while Ben was just doing it. Dick's mind was busy trying to understand the right way to turn, consciously directing his body through it step by step, and then analyzing the results. After each "mistake" he criticized himself harshly and strained even harder. Ben, on the other hand, watched what others were doing and simply imitated them. He wasn't trying to analyze how to turn, or worrying about doing it the right way or about looking good. Since he was just out to ski and have fun, he did both without strain, whereas Dick was trying too hard to have fun and too busy talking to himself to learn much.

How often have you watched—with a mixture of wonder and resentment—"those damn kids" on their little skis shoot down the beginners' slope, weaving in and out between older beginners? The first time they strap on a pair of skis, children seem to have an innate sense about the sport.

While the rest of us are still stiffly snowplowing our way across a slope, they have been up and down it five times.

Children are natural learners. Psychologists and learning theorists tell us that we learn more in our first five years than we are apt to absorb during the rest of our lives. Why? Do children know something that we don't? Have we forgotten something we once knew?

Children learn faster because they don't think they know anything to start with. Ben didn't have any preconceived ideas about the right way to ski. He simply went out on a slope, watched others and tried to duplicate what he saw, letting his body find out what worked best. His mind was clear and open to discovery.

Dick's mind, on the other hand, was too full of the rights and wrongs, the dos and don'ts of skiing, to be open to learning. Talking his way down the mountain, he skied more with his head than with his body. All his self-instructions prevented him from experiencing his skis and his body.

Conceptual Learning: Trying to Do It the "Right" Way

I remember attending as an adolescent one of those dance classes where we learned the box step by moving our feet from one footprint to the next, chanting "Forward, across, together, back, across, together . . ." After practicing to this rigid cadence, music was finally played and we were expected to pick out a partner and start dancing.

However, any similarity between what I was doing and real dancing was purely coincidental. I would step all over my partner's feet as I counted "One, Two, Three, forward, back, together," making sure that my feet were in the "right" place.

Most adults try to learn by memorizing a series of individual actions to create one whole movement. Hence, their approach to skiing is to follow footprints in their minds. Initially they look outside themselves—perhaps a magazine article, an instructor or a not-so-knowledgeable friend—for a set of concepts of the "right" way to ski. They focus their attention on those concepts, doing everything they can to follow them, not realizing that by intellectualizing the process they are stifling the sense of their bodies' movements. Ben did exactly the opposite, which is why he learned so easily.

When I was a beginner, the "correct" way to ski was to keep your legs tightly pressed together with your boots touching. In all the instructional manuals the emphasis was on making parallel turns and keeping the body in this position. If you had your skis close together, you were good; if not, thumbs down. All my efforts were guided by this concept of how I should be skiing, and I never focused on how my body responded to it or whether it actually worked for me or not. At first, it felt uncomfortable and unnatural. But I wasn't concerned with how my body was feeling because I wanted so badly to do it right. After years of forcing my legs and skis into this position, the discomfort was almost unnoticeable—not because it became natural but because it became habit. I was aware not of how I felt but of how I thought I looked.

Learning by following rules, we judge our performance on the basis of how close it is to the "right way." The conceptualized turn is good not because it feels right and works, but only because it conforms to the standard. However, if we allow a concept to guide our experience, we perform by rote, and our actions are mechanical and unnatural. Our learning is impeded because we are no longer being led by experience but by ideas. As a result, Self 2 is screened off from feeling the necessary subtleties of our actions and is therefore prevented from developing any refinements.

It is more important to feel where your skis are than to know where they should be. If you are obsessed with shoulds to the point of neglecting what is, you will soon be frustrated, angry and discouraged—none of this will help your performance. The child, on the other hand, knows what he wants to do and has no preconceived notions about the right way of doing it.

"Should" is a concept of the way things aren't instead of the way they are. The player of the Inner Game often finds that the right way is the wrong way. He may use concepts to point him in a certain direction, but he relies on his experience of what feels good and at the same time works best for him. In the Inner Game the should emerges spontaneously as we increase our awareness of is.

Many people, myself included, were guided for years by the shoulds of parents, friends and society: the right way of doing things, the right profession, the right life style, the right relationship. Rather than letting our own intuition, awareness and interests guide our choices, we conformed, but many of us failed to find fulfillment.

47

Experiential Learning

Billy's mother points to the fireplace and says, "See that fire? Be careful of it because it's very hot and can burn you badly. Stay away from it!" Tommy's mother leads him close to the fire, holds his hand out toward it and says, "Now, move a little closer." Tommy does so, but stops at the point where the heat becomes too uncomfortable. "Hot," his mother says as he withdraws his hand. "Fire is hot, and if you get too close it burns you."

On being *told* about the dangers of fire, the first child tucks the idea into his mind and has to remind himself whenever he is near fire not to get close to it. By being allowed to *feel* the heat and discover the danger for himself, Tommy *knows* through experience that fire is hot and he will exercise caution. Billy learned only that his mother didn't want him near the fire, while Tommy learned that the danger of the heat depended on how close he came to the fire. Billy learned to fear fire, while Tommy learned to respect it, so that his mind will be open to discovering its uses and appreciating its beauty.

To have to try to remember something means that you don't really *know* it. Because his mind is so full of other thoughts and ideas, sooner or later Billy won't remember his mother's caution; eventually he will get a little too close, feel the heat and *then* will learn about fire the hard way.

When you are aware of an experience, you learn at a level much deeper than that of the conceptual

48

mind. Awareness is the Self 2 learning process, whereas conceptual learning starts and stops at Self 1. Moreover, almost any action is far more complex than any description of it. The art of skiing can't be described as the act of keeping knees bent and skis together, any more than fire can be described by just saying that it's hot. An action is a synthesis of many movements, all executed in harmony with one another. It would be impossible for the mind to learn by rote all the intricacies of movement involved in turning your skis, let alone sending all those instructions simultaneously to the muscles of your body so that you can accomplish that turn.

Self 2 learns by discovery—by *doing* rather than *thinking about doing*. Like an explorer, Self 2 always perceives its environment as virgin territory. With a childlike curiosity, it is open and attentive to whatever it may encounter. It may have a preliminary idea of where it wants to go and what it wants to accomplish, but it is free of constricting expectations of how its goal must be achieved or what it will find on its way.

Self 2 lets experience be the guide. Remaining objective and interested, it grows by absorbing what is happening from moment to moment. In the process of discovery it senses and observes, constantly picking up information and making appropriate adjustments in its actions and direction, thus becoming increasingly able to cope with the situation at hand. The natural learning process is discovery by experience.

Gawking

When my son Otis is exposed to an unfamiliar skill, he will watch what is going on for a few minutes with total concentration. Wide-eyed, he simply gawks, absorbing the entire image at once without breaking it down into its separate parts. It is because children don't segment experience that they are such superb mimics.

The adult, on the other hand, tends to see movement in terms of a series of stop-action poses which he then translates into a list of instructions to himself. "Oh, I see—he edges his downhill ski, plants his pole, steps onto the uphill ski and rides it through the turn." Even if he were to succeed in forcing his body to comply with these instructions, he would miss much of what a skiing turn is. A turn is more than just the sum of its parts; it includes rhythm, grace, balance and coordination—none of which is on Self 1's list. Skiing by the numbers usually results in moving like a robot through the turn.

A child doesn't learn linearly; he learns holistically. With a quiet and open mind, he takes in whole images: not just visual images, but "feelages" as well. With his concentration focused, he acquires a *feel* for what he is seeing. Self 2 then creates corresponding kinesthetic sensations in his body, so that he is almost duplicating the movement as he watches it. Free of self-judgments, when he begins to move he imitates what he saw.

Totally involved in his actions, his senses continually feed back detailed information from the experience.

A baby may fall when first attempting to walk, but when he does, his body absorbs all the details of the fall. Without concepts of any kind, his Self 2 automatically adjusts the next step he takes, making it longer or shorter, straightening the position of the head to correct for imbalance. As his body continues to receive more detailed information with each succeeding step, it is able to refine the new movement. Only because his mind is quiet enough to feel the subtle sensations that tell him when he is on or off balance does any learning take place.

This demonstrates a basic principle of the Inner Game, and the essence of the natural learning process: *the quality of learning is directly proportionate to the quality of feedback one receives from experience.* A mind that is busy worrying, criticizing and comparing will block feedback, just as a clogged filter will prevent air from flowing through it. The more active the mind, the less feedback the body will receive and the slower it will learn. The key to natural learning is to quiet the mind so that awareness is increased.

Body Awareness

While skiing, we get visual feedback from the terrain and aural feedback from the sounds our skis make on the snow. However, we learn most from

51

our awareness of the movements of the body. Learning increases in direct proportion to our ability to focus on this.

What does body awareness mean? Try this simple exercise and experience it for yourself. Raise your right hand over your head. Then lower it. Raise it a second time, but this time notice how it feels as you are lifting it. Experience your hand lowering again. What was the difference between the two sets of movement? Lift your arm a third time with your eyes shut so you can more easily focus on the feeling. How can you tell that your arm is actually moving? What sensations indicate the location of your arm at each moment? Can you distinguish between the sensations of upward and downward movements? If you pay close attention, you will feel some muscles tighten while others relax at the moment the arm changes directions. See if you can locate those muscles which contract in order to raise the arm. Can you feel them let go as the arm lowers?

The more attentive and relaxed the mind, the more able it is to pick up increasingly minute muscle and energy sensations in the body. Continue the exercise with other parts of the body. You will find that the more attentive the mind grows, the more subtle sensations it will pick up.

Frequently, after a skier makes a few turns and I ask him what he experienced, the answer comes back in terms of what *wasn't* experienced. For example: "I didn't plant my pole right."

"How do you know you didn't plant your pole right?"

"Because it didn't feel right."

"What did you actually feel that told you it wasn't right?"

"My arm felt rigid and my shoulder was tight."

"Aha! Then *that's* the experience. You felt the rigidity in your arm and the tightness in your shoulder. Everything else you reported was only thinking."

Awareness is experiencing something directly; *thinking* is to conceptualize about what we are experiencing. They are two critically different processes. The more we think about an experience, the less aware we become of the experience itself. Once again: *as thinking increases, awareness decreases.*

If, while listening to a person who is talking to me, I look at him directly and attend to his words, I will be aware of the essential communication between us. But if I am wondering how he feels about me, or if I am busily preparing my reply to what he is saying, I am obviously not going to be aware of what is being communicated by him.

Two Examples

One day Tim Gallwey was asked to demonstrate to a group of ski instructors how Inner Game principles might be applied to the teaching of novice skiers. First he observed a beginners' class as it was being taught, and then he was given a class of twelve students who had never been on skis before. It would be his first group of students off the tennis courts, and he was obviously looking forward to the experiment.

The first step with beginners at this particular school was to teach them how to side-step up a hill. Tim followed this procedure, but gave no instructions about how each step should be done. Once the class had their skis on, he simply asked the students while standing still to get used to the extensions on their feet. He suggested that they shift their weight from one foot to the other, move them up and down and sideways, bend and straighten their knees, and edge and flatten their skis. Each pupil explored in his own way what it was like to wear skis. There were no rights or wrongs, simply the exploration of something new. After a few minutes Tim said, "Follow me," and started side-stepping up the gentle slope. Before the novices could start worrying about whether they were following him "correctly," Tim started talking. "The first thing I want you to become aware of is your skis. As you move up the hill, are they flat or edged into the snow? Don't look at mine and don't look at your own. I simply want you to feel them."

The students immediately stopped trying to side-step and began to become aware of their skis. As they progressed up the hill, each of them could tell that his skis were edged into the snow. Then, partway up the slope, Tim stopped them and asked them to play with their edges some more. "Without looking at them, see what happens when you flatten your skis." As the students did so, they all began to slide a little downhill, then automatically edged to stop themselves. "That's why you were all edging as you side-stepped," he said. "Who told you how to do that? I didn't; yet everyone did it. In a traditional class, you might have been told to remember to edge your skis, and you probably would have tried hard to do it 'right.' But now you are doing it automatically

54

without thinking about it. Something in you is pretty smart, and as you learn to ski you will grow to trust it more and more.

"Next, I want you to edge your skis as much as you possibly can. . . . We'll call that amount of edging a five. Now a little less—that's four—still less—that's three—and perfectly flat will be zero. Now as we continue to side-step up the hill, I want each of you to call out the number which corresponds to the degree that you feel your skis are edged into the snow. There's no correct number; just feel how much they are edged, step by step, and call out the number. Remember, no fair looking—just do it by feel." As the students started up the slope, calling out numbers, it was easy to see that their concentration had increased. There was no anxiety in their voices, simply absorption in what they were feeling. At first the numbers varied from about one to four, but after a while each student seemed to have found his particular number. At the top of the rise Tim stopped the class and asked each member to report the amount of edging he was using most. Most had settled on a two or three, and one girl asked if three was "best." "I don't know which number is best," said Tim. "How did you find that three worked?" "Oh, it worked fine," said the girl. "I just didn't know if it was right." Tim's comment was, "It's obviously right for you at this moment."

Everyone looked relieved that this hadn't been a test. They seemed to be getting the idea that this teacher trusted them to discover what worked best for each of them. Without really trying they had already learned side-stepping, simple control of skis, and a basic awareness of edging which would form a foundation for their skiing.

I saw how simple yet universally applicable this principle of body awareness was the next day, when Tim was working with a group of advanced skiers. Among these was Peter, an instructor from Zermatt, who had been teaching skiing for twenty years. Four of us took a run down an intermediate slope with no instruction other than to be aware of our bodies and to notice which part held our attention the most. After skiing half the run, each of us reported what we had focused on. My attention had centered on my knees as I had become interested in the extent they were bending on each turn. Tim had been most aware of the rotation of his shoulders. When it was Peter's turn to report, he seemed slightly bored. "Vell, I am alvays avare ov my edges ven I ski," he said. He seemed so competent and self-assured that I began to wonder if Inner Skiing could possibly offer him anything.

Then Tim said that he wanted to pay even closer attention to his shoulders, and suggested that each of us simply increase our awareness of the part of our bodies that had come to our attention. I was amused when he suggested to Peter exactly what he had told the class of beginners the day before. "Peter, you seem to focus on your edges, but why don't you see if you can increase your awareness. Call the maximum amount of edging ten and zero for flat. As you take each turn call out to yourself the number that seems right to you."

When we collected at the bottom of the slope, Peter was so excited that I could hardly understand all that he said. "It was vonderful! I never felt quite like that. I could tell such little differences. Ven I vas at seven it was like pure light, and then ven I unedged at zero, the darkness was there. It vas beautiful."

The reference to light and darkness puzzled us, but we could all tell that Peter, who had skied all his life and seemed beyond any surprise, was now like a kid with a new toy. He was discovering the secret of awareness, and how it makes all experience fresh. What we all found out was that simple body awareness is the same for everyone. We never outgrow it. Only the degree of subtlety increases.

Feedback from Results

Natural learning depends on more than feedback from the body; it also depends on what *works*. Not all the moves in skiing will feel natural at first because our bodies were designed for walking and running, not for sliding across snow at high speeds. When working with the beginners, Tim emphasized focusing not only on the subtle sensations of the body but also on results. He encouraged them to be able to feel the difference between a three and a zero edge, and also to observe the different *effects* of each amount of edging.

Only by getting accurate feedback from both the feel of muscle movements and the results of these movements can Self 2 make the appropriate corrections. If the skier is trying too hard to attain certain results, it will be far more difficult for him to feel those that he is achieving, which in turn will interfere with the correction process. If he makes a certain movement which causes him to fall, he needn't try to make a conscious correction. If he felt both the movement causing the imbalance and the resulting fall, the automatic learning process of Self 2 will make the correction. Although this may be hard to believe for those who have become used to trusting only their conscious Self 1, a little experimenting will prove that the body really does know how to correct itself if it is given the necessary feedback.

When Tim is teaching tennis students to hit targets with their serve, he always says that it's not necessary to try to hit the target; rather, what is important is to see exactly where each serve lands in relation to the target. If the student misses the target by five feet to the right, he isn't asked to aim farther to the left, but he is simply told to serve again without consciously trying to make any correction. His Self 2 is trusted to do the correcting. Self 1 is always surprised when it sees how soon the body learns to hit the target without its help.

The same principle is applicable to skiing. I need to feel what happens when my skis flatten coming out of a turn, when they are slightly edged and when they are more edged. By increasing awareness of both my edging and its effects on the quality of the turn, Self 2 soon discovers the optimum relationship between the two. Since there is such a wide range in terrain and speed, this optimum relationship will vary greatly.

One might well ask, "But what is the *target* in skiing?" Although the desirable goal in skiing may not be as clear-cut as in sports like tennis and golf where you keep score, it can still be recognized. To maintain *balance* while skiing—on any terrain and at any speed—is one of many ways to describe the target. Balance is necessary in all movement and the body has a particularly strong desire to achieve it when skiing. It knows much better than the conceptual mind, Self 1, how to achieve this goal.

Awareness Increases Control

Many skiers assume that if they neglect technical information in favor of increasing body awareness, they will sacrifice proficiency. But the reverse is true. The complex feedback we get from awareness of our bodies is much more subtle and refined than the most carefully worded verbal instructions. Who can describe in words the exact amount of edging which produces the most effective turn in a given situation? The language of the body is simply too specific and sophisticated to be put into words. But we can learn that language, if we listen to our bodies, and attend to the subtleties of our kinesthetic sensations.

Increasing our ability to focus on our body sensations while skiing takes some practice. The primary purpose of the exercise is to quiet Self 1, to limit conscious thought and to feel what is happening to our bodies. There are many ways to facilitate this process. Below are two that I have found beneficial.

A few years ago, while I was skiing at Lake Eldora, Tom Walker, the ski school director, asked me to try taking a few turns with my eyes closed. I looked around. The area was relatively flat and nobody was in sight, so I nervously agreed. But when I tried it I was so tense and afraid that all I was aware of was my mind racing in panic. Self 1 kept saying, "Watch out! You're heading for trouble!" As a result, I took only two cautious turns before opening my eyes and smiling sheepishly.

"Want to try again?" Tom asked. "It usually takes a few times to get accustomed to it."

This time I was more able to relax, and soon I became acutely aware of my feet. They seemed at one with my skis, and I could actually feel each minute change in the terrain beneath them. Even after I opened my eyes, this increased sense of awareness stayed with me, and it led to a degree of control I had never before achieved. I became aware of the slightest change in angle my edges made, my body seemed to know just how much to edge, and I was carving turns with greater precision and less effort than I had ever imagined possible.

Later Tom suggested that I take a run with my boots unbuckled. I was surprised because I had always thought that one's boots needed to be tight in order to gain maximum control. Somewhat skeptical, I started out tentatively, but it turned out to be a valuable experience. I was prevented from making any sudden movements to execute a turn because my feet would have come out of my boots; it became necessary to focus more on the soles of my feet and allow them to control my skis. I noticed how much more aware I was of the slightest change in pressure, and noticed how much control I achieved by attending to these subtle differences. Barely moving my body, simply by pressuring my feet, I could make the skis do almost anything I wanted.

In some segments of Japanese and Chinese society, small children are introduced to one or another of the martial arts, which emphasize alertness to subtle body sensations. In T'ai Chi Ch'uan, for instance, every movement is made carefully and slowly in order to increase one's awareness of actions and of the delicate flow of energy throughout the body. A T'ai Chi master attains an amazing level of agility and control, the inevitable and natural by-products of awareness.

In our own culture, achievement is valued over awareness, as though they were independent of each other, when in point of fact body awareness is directly related to body achievement. In any sport the athletes who possess an acute ability to focus on the discrete signals of their bodies—for example, the fine line between balance and imbalance, timing and mistiming, being too tight and too loose—are those who achieve excellence.

The will to strive for higher levels of achievement is valuable, and has been the greatest spur to the development of sports in the Western world, but I feel that we have so overstressed our emphasis on this goal that a reassessment in favor of awareness is needed. Pure awareness without the will to achieve lacks direction, but the will to achieve without awareness is strained and lacks the requisite refinement to attain the highest levels of excellence. The human body is a magnificent instrument that constantly sends us subtle messages; if heeded, these would keep us healthy and allow us to perform at our highest level. But when we become too goal-oriented and anxious about the results of our actions, we begin to lose touch with our bodies. When we lack awareness of its messages, immediately our performance suffers.

To increase control over one's body, we must resist any tendency to force change. In the Inner Game approach to learning, growth begins by increasing our awareness of that which we wish to change.

Through heightened awareness, people have learned to achieve surprising degrees of control over their bodies—to slow down their heartbeat, decrease their blood pressure and hasten their digestion. I once participated in an experiment whose goal was to raise the temperature of one's fingertips. My fingers were hooked up to a galvanic skin-response meter. Attempting to increase their temperature, I concentrated on thinking about the sun shining on my fingers, and then of putting my hands in a furnace. The result was a *decrease* of five points. Next I imagined putting my fingers in hot water, and then I tried to send heat to them through my bloodstream. Nothing worked.

The experimenter came over to me and asked, "Can you feel the temperature your hands are at now?"

"No."

"Start with that and see what happens."

Closing my eyes, I shifted my attention to the tips of my fingers, focusing on feeling what their temperature was, rather than on trying to force it up. Soon I could feel subtle changes occurring. Although I wasn't consciously trying to reach my goal, I became aware that my fingers were starting to heat up. When I opened my eyes, the temperature had increased five points! Within a short time, I was able to increase or decrease their temperature at will.

Heightened awareness leads to increased control at all levels of skiing. The more advanced one is, the greater the need for increasingly refined awareness in order to make the fine adjustments necessary to achieve balance and control at higher speeds. Nowhere is this more evident than with racers shooting through slalom courses. Since the first five places are often separated only by tenths of a second, the competitors must ski with the highest degree of precision. Even the most minute degree of over or under edging can alter the racer's line through a gate and not only cost him the race but send him shooting off the course.

Richard Bach describes how Jonathan Livingston Seagull, having learned to dive at 214 miles an hour, realizes the importance of subtle body awareness as he tries to discover how to turn at high speed:

> A single wingtip feather, he found, moved a fraction of an inch, gives a smooth sweeping curve at tremendous speed. Before he learned this, however, he found that moving more than one feather at that speed will spin you like a rifle ball. . . .

Judging: An Obstacle to Awareness

Perhaps the most important step a person can take to increase awareness of his experience, on the mountain or off, is to let go of the habit of judging himself or his skiing in terms of good and bad.

In assessing the turn you have just made, you are paying too much attention to past history, and this numbs you to what is happening in the present. In brooding over that turn, you are not feeling your body or your skis right now, and you don't see clearly the terrain in front of you. Consequently you fall a little behind, and don't react quickly enough to the feedback from the turn being made because you are not "there." When the turn is labeled "good," Self 1 congratulates you and tries to remember exactly what you did so that you can repeat it. But, of course, that is not how you made the "good" turn in the first place, nor how you will make the next. After pronouncing a turn "bad," Self 1 bawls you out, starts to analyze what went wrong, and tries to force a correction. Hence "good" is no more effective than "bad," since both judgments cause you to strain either to repeat or to remedy. Self 2 needs detailed feedback from the last turn to make its corrections—not a judgment.

If you've ever bowled, you've probably seen someone turn away disgustedly as soon as he sees that his shot is not going to hit all ten pins. He doesn't want to see how bad his ball actually was, so he learns little. Can you imagine a skier who never fell? The experiences which we call mistakes are actually valuable feedback which our bodies need in order to discriminate between what works for us and what doesn't and to make the appropriate corrections.

Errors are an integral part of the learning process, even for experts. Regardless of the level at which you ski, you will make mistakes, but you can benefit from them. What we need to eliminate is not the mistakes themselves, but our fear of making them and the consequent judgments, criticisms and anger. By accepting errors we usually make fewer of them. Further, though we may begin by only judging our performance, we generally end up judging ourselves. Accusations have a momentum of their own. Not shifting our weight quickly enough causes a "bad" turn, which creates negative feelings and often results in a "bad" run, and this, in turn, causes more negative feelings. This can easily lead to a "bad" day, and after a few such "bad" days we conclude that we are "bad" skiers. This discouragement and frustration often lingers on long after we have left the mountain, turning us into "bad" people.

Such self-judgment distorts perception, interferes with performance and retards our abilities to learn and perform. The skier who decides that he is having a bad day inevitably will have one. The person who decides that he has reached a plateau will stay there until he decides that he is off it.

There are no bad skiers—only skiers at different levels of physical and mental development. A flower is not "better" when it blooms than when it was a bud, it is simply at a different level of development. When we stop judging ourselves and others, we become more willing to trust ourselves and we begin to ski more freely and naturally.

As Hamlet said to Rosencrantz and Guildenstern, "There's nothing either good or bad but thinking makes it so."

Mistrust

Another obstacle to awareness and natural learning is mistrust of one's Self 2. The more a skier doubts his natural ability, the more he will instruct himself and try hard. Also, it is difficult to be aware of feedback when Self 1 is trying to force your body to do what you doubt that it can do on its own.

Since keeping balance is essential to skiing well at all levels, it is pertinent to ask whether Self 1 or Self 2 should be entrusted with this task. We've all had the experience of catching an edge or hitting a bump and being thrown off balance. We teeter in the air, suspended in space as we ride on one ski but then an arm or leg flies out in the opposite direction and we manage to regain our upright position. It happens so fast that we react without thinking—without even realizing what we've done. In the instant we lose our balance Self 2 automatically makes five, ten, twenty-five or more adjustments to keep us upright. Can Self 1 direct you with that much sophistication?

Rock Dancing

As we learn to trust the body and stop trying to control and direct it, we begin to experience amazing results.

At the last meeting of a one-year teacher-training project I was directing, our group decided to take a week-long backpacking and climbing trip in the Sierras. We planned to climb one of the higher peaks as part of the trip. Starting out early one morning, we made it to the top by noon. It was an exhausting climb. After a picnic of wine and cheese and much elation, we started down.

At one point we hit a stretch of huge boulders and began jumping from one to the next. Gradually we picked up speed, and soon we were going so fast that there was no time to think about which rock to jump to next or how to land. We had to abandon our desire for conscious control and simply trust our bodies as we flew down the mountain. My attention was so riveted on what I was doing that there was no thought between awareness and action, between the feeling and doing. At first it was a little frightening, but when I saw that my body knew what it was doing, I began to trust it even more, and my fear gave way to exhilaration. It was as if I was just along for the ride on a roller coaster, unable to control its momentum even if I had wanted to. I was out of my mind.

It seems a paradox that in order to gain real control we have to let go of trying to achieve control. But it simply means abandoning Self 1's control and letting Self 2 take over. As the Zen archer says, "We don't shoot the arrow; it shoots itself."

Before a skier can hope to achieve control, he must confront and overcome what is for most the greatest single mental obstacle to progress in skiing: fear.

4

Fear of Falling, Failing and Flying

Two Kinds of Fear

At an Inner Skiing workshop Tim and I were conducting we asked the three hundred participants to name the inner obstacles which most interfered with their proficiency and enjoyment of skiing, and then to rate these barriers by applauding to the degree that they shared them. Listening to the length and volume of the applause, we rated the obstacles on a scale from one to ten—ten being the most common and difficult, and one being those that presented a relatively low degree of difficulty.

Among other difficulties mentioned were negative self-image, poor concentration, trying too hard and too many self-instructions. Most of these rated from three to seven on the applause meter. But fear got a thirteen; it went off the scale! There were very few participants who didn't feel that this emotion was at least detrimental to their skiing, and most saw it as a major problem. Some people in the audience even said that because of fear they had never before wanted to learn how to ski.

Tim's next announcement that the second part of the program would deal with this mental obstacle was met with cheers. It seemed to both of us that most of the participants were hoping for a magical cure—something that would immediately end their fear and create instant courage.

However, Tim took a more comprehensive approach. He asked, "Is all fear bad? Isn't there a kind of fear that isn't harmful, but in fact helpful? Haven't most of you been in a real emergency when, instead of panicking, you felt a rush of adrenaline, knew exactly what to do and did it? This reaction is also called fear, but rather than hindering us, it helps us do things which in normal circumstances we think are well beyond our capabilities.

"Chased by a bull in a field, a lady who had never done anything athletic might run a hundred yards in twelve seconds and leap a four-foot fence without ever pausing to doubt that she could do it. Not until she was safe would she remember that she was a slow runner and couldn't jump fences.

"Although we call this kind of response 'fear,' it is markedly different from what happens to most of us as we stand atop a mountain, shaking in our boots as we look down at a mogul field, imagining all the different ways that we might fall. It's strange that we call these two responses by the same name. One heightens our perceptions and gives us added energy to perform beyond our normal capacities, whereas the other distorts our perceptions, tending to paralyze us and decrease our competence. We need only work at decreasing this second fear; the first is welcome."

When I was eighteen years old, I experienced vividly the contrasting effects of these two fears one summer while I was a lifeguard at Rockaway

Beach on Long Island. It was the day after a hurricane and the waves were mountainous. Judging that the ocean was too dangerous for the average swimmer, the other lifeguards and I closed the beach to public swimming. Being strong swimmers ourselves, however, we decided to challenge the waves. It was a memorable experience for all of us, but especially for me. Catching one of those waves was like riding down a fifteen-foot slide with power behind it. When we were wiped out and thrown to the ocean floor, we would wait for a second while the wave passed over us and then push up toward the surface. The worst that could happen, we thought, would be a mouthful of salt water or a scraped nose.

Once, however, as I started toward the surface after a wipe-out, my legs became entangled in a safety rope which had come loose from its mooring. I struggled to free myself from it, but the rope only got tighter, making it impossible for me to work my way to the surface. I tried to use the rope to pull myself up, but just as I got my head above the surface for a gulp of air a huge wave crashed down on me, filling my mouth with water and pushing me to the bottom again.

I started to panic. I couldn't see, my lungs were bursting, and I felt my strength ebbing. I began to think I was going to drown. No matter how hard I tried, I couldn't get free of the rope. In one more desperate attempt, I yanked on it as hard as I could, but it only tightened more.

Luckily, something else suddenly took over. I felt an onrush of energy, my panic subsided and I grew very calm. I knew I was in serious danger, but I stopped struggling blindly. Time seemed to slow and everything became clear. Without thinking, I knew intuitively what to do. Exhaling the remaining air in my lungs, I relaxed my muscles and let myself drop toward the ocean floor. As I descended I felt the rope loosen slightly around my legs, so that when I hit the bottom I was able to disentangle myself, push off strongly and shoot to the top.

Caught in the initial fear, all my thrashing had only got me deeper into trouble, almost costing me my life. Even though I was in greater danger by the time the second fear took over, my mind was calmer and my efforts more appropriate to the situation. I actually had more air and more strength left than my fear had led me to believe. Once free of panic, I found it easy to free myself.

Since these two kinds of fear have such distinct effects on perception and performance, it makes sense to call them by different names and to learn to distinguish between them. Fear 2 will be examined first because it emerges only in rare or abnormal situations; also, it serves as a useful contrast to Fear 1, the primary obstacle for most skiers.

Fear 2

When confronted with an emergency situation, the human body undergoes a series of physiological adjustments which prepare it for heightened action. Adrenaline is secreted into the bloodstream and breathing is stimulated. The chest expands and the throat relaxes to handle the increase of air intake. Pulse and blood pressure increase, as does the volume of blood sent to the muscles of the arms and legs. The liver manufactures glucose, adding fuel to the tissues, and the pupils of the eyes dilate, sharpening visual perception. In these amazing ways the body prepares itself for peak performance. This is the helpful kind of fear, and since it is wholly a function of Self 2 it will be referred to hereafter as Fear 2.

Fear 2 is the body's natural response to challenge. It can exist simultaneously with courage, and often precedes the performances of athletes, actors, race car drivers, soldiers or anyone in a high-risk situation. I know a man of ordinary size who, responding to a cry of alarm, found his son with his leg caught under the wheel of a car. Without hesitation and with a powerful surge of energy, he lifted the front end of the car, freeing his son's leg.

Fear 2 focuses our attention in the present and lends us capabilities beyond our normal levels. Since this kind of fear is helpful to us, we need to learn not to resist it, nor to waste the energy it produces.

Fear 1

The fear that *is* harmful because it interferes with our abilities to perform at our best originates in the imagination of Self 1, the ego mind, and so will be called Fear 1.

Fear 1 has a magnifying effect on our perceptions. When looking at danger, it greatly enlarges what it sees. Medium-sized bumps become *giant moguls*, intermediate slopes become *sheer preci-*

pices, the possibility of falling becomes a broken leg.

While our perception of danger is exaggerated by seeing it through the small end of the telescope, our abilities to cope with this danger seem to shrink, as if we were looking through the opposite end. Our sense of competence is so depleted that we feel powerless to handle the situation confronting us.

The combined effects of these distortions make an intermediate skier at the top of an intermediate slope perceive it as advanced and himself as a beginner. Confused by these illusions, the skier, instead of reacting with heightened capabilities as he might under the influence of Fear 2, responds with hesitance and overcautiousness, which can ultimately induce paralysis.

Standing at the head of a trail, the skier in the grip of Fear 1 looks down and begins to think how steep it looks. Feeling the anxiety churning in his stomach, he thinks of the times he has fallen on similar slopes or in similar conditions. He may remember a time when he was hurt and see it happening again. Instead of flexing slightly in readiness for action, his muscles react to his fear by becoming rigid and immobile. His courage ebbs, he feels weaker and his vision blurs.

The more the skier's anxiety mounts, the more Self 1 inflates the danger and deflates his ability. If eventually he does attempt the slope, he does so with overtight muscles and in a distracted state. He is so sure that he is going to fall that indeed he does, even before moving very fast. He picks himself up embarrassed, knowing at this point that the slope wasn't difficult and that there was no need to fall. By exaggerating the danger and minimizing his own capabilities, Fear 1 caused his negative expectations to materialize.

This tendency of Fear 1 to magnify perceptions, to make things seem worse than they are, occurs in many areas of life. Many years ago I applied for a job with a New York advertising agency, and was told to wait in the reception room until I was called. Joining the other applicants and feeling very nervous, I peeked over my magazine to look at the competition. They were all Gregory Pecks, self-assured and calm. I began to think how much better dressed and how much more professional they looked. Soon I was a nervous wreck—my hands sweating, stomach queasy—and became so caught up in the fear I had created for myself that it was difficult to be at my best when my interview took place.

The Effect of Fear 1 on Our Skiing

The mind and the body are not separate units working independently; each affects the other. Originating in the mind, Fear 1 is immediately transmitted to the body and governs its actions.

Probably the most vivid examples of its results in skiing can be seen with beginners. Their most common characteristic is stiffness of movement. Their legs tend to be tight and inflexible, their knees locked, their shoulders hunched, their fists clenched tight as they hold their poles and their faces scrunched grimly. Fear 1 can transform a class of novices into petrified statues being pushed across a slope.

When muscles are overly tense, they lose flexibility and can't react smoothly to changes in the terrain. While skiing, our knees and hips are meant to act as shock absorbers, compressing to cushion the jarring effect of bumps and then returning to normal. If these shock absorbers are already compressed, they will have no flexibility with which to react to differences in the terrain. Skiing would then be like riding over a rough road in an old jeep: every small bump reverberates through our bodies, and the larger ones bounce us off the seat, throwing us off balance.

Besides inhibiting our flexibility, the tension resulting from Fear 1 also reduces our stamina. When our bodies are tight we have to work harder: every muscle we tense or flex requires extra effort. As our energy reserves are depleted, we tire more quickly. Our reactions slow down, our sense of timing is thrown off, our muscles become exhausted and we lose control. As a result, our self-doubts and fears build, and the cycle perpetuates itself.

On the other hand, when we are relaxed and are skiing with Self 2 effort, we employ only the necessary muscles, and no energy is wasted in the over-tightness that comes from fear and forcing. The upper body—stomach, arms, shoulders, neck and face muscles—is relatively loose, and the leg muscles do most of the skiing.

Another effect of Fear 1 is that it literally takes our breath away: we tend to stop breathing. To demonstrate the effects of this, I often ask members of my classes to hold their breath while running in place as fast as they can for one minute, paying attention to how their bodies feel while doing so. Then I ask them to run in place again, at the same speed and for the same period of time, breathing normally. Holding their breaths, they tire much more quickly—literally running out of steam. Holding one's breath not only results in unnecessary tightness of the torso and face but causes loss of oxygen. In contrast, Fear 2 induces the opposite effect, increasing the oxygen intake of the body.

The "Uh-oh" Experience

In *Inner Tennis*, Tim describes a common cause of error on the courts as the "uh-oh" experience. A player with a strong forehand will return with confidence a ball coming toward his right, but when he has to use his weak backhand, he says to himself, "Uh-oh." In response to this warning, his arm tightens, his racket is jerked out of its natural path, the ball is hit off center and an error results.

This self-induced failure applies to other sports as well. Take the example of someone who has skied for a year but who still thinks of himself as a beginner. The instant he pushes off downhill he feels unsure of himself and moves overcautiously. Afraid of losing the slightest degree of control, as he starts to pick up any speed he thinks, Uh-oh, I'm going too fast. To resist forward momentum he sits backward, thereby weighting the tails of his skis, which causes him to go even faster and to lose still more control. Uh-oh, here comes a fall, he thinks, sitting still further back, thus accelerating more and tightening his body in anticipation of the fall.

I knew that was going to happen! I'm a lousy skier, he says to himself, further reinforcing his negative self-image. I'm still falling all over the beginners' slope. Now he has one more memory with which to further distort his true competence and feed Fear 1. The next time he picks up speed, his fear again will cause him to tighten and lean back again for a repeat performance.

The Fear I Cycle

Illusion-based fear operates in a simple, self-destructive cycle. We look at a mogul field and think, I'm not good enough to handle that. The moguls begin to grow in size and degree of difficulty, and this distorted perception affects the body, which tenses in anticipation of being hurt. With muscles tight, our movements are stiff, and indeed a mogul does throw us up just as we imagined it would. This distortion in performance reinforces our already distorted self-image, and the next mogul will look even larger and more difficult.

Fear 1 distorts each component of our skiing: our perception, our performance and our self-image. Each distortion reflects its own illusions, further skewing each of the other components. This fear cycle will inevitably continue until the distortions on which it is based are broken.

Overcoming Fear 1

Awareness Dispels Illusion

The essential difference between Fear 2 and Fear 1 is that Fear 2 is based on reality, whereas Fear 1 is based on illusion. There is only one way to dispel illusion: to increase one's awareness of reality —of what really *is*. Though there are many ways to change the *shape* of an illusion, only awareness can *eliminate* it.

Awareness is light; illusion is darkness. Nothing except light can take away darkness. Illusion means seeing things which aren't there, or not seeing things which are there. Awareness is the energy of consciousness which, when focused on reality, allows us to see only what *is*.

A young boy going to sleep is sure he sees a boogeyman in the darkened bedroom and is paralyzed with terror. This illusion has a very real power until his father, answering the boy's frightened cries, comes in and turns on the light. The boy peeks out from under his covers, looks in the direction of the boogeyman and sees only his own clothes draped over a chair.

"I thought I saw a boogeyman," he says sheepishly.

"Well, now you can see that there's no one here," the father says as he leaves.

But the father is wrong. There *was* a boogeyman in the room: the Fear 1 in the child's imagination—which more than likely is also still alive and well in the father's. Until the inner boogeyman is confronted, the one which projects its fears onto our external reality, we all live in the dark.

How to turn on the lights? How does one go about increasing awareness of what is in order to decrease Fear 1?

The Three Components of Fear 1

There are only three essential components in every fear situation, and Self 1 projects its illusions on any or all of them to produce Fear 1. First, there is the sense of *danger*—that is, something capable of doing harm. Second, there is the sense of *vulnerability*—that is, there is someone capable of being harmed by this danger. Third, there is a sense of *inability* on the part of the vulnerable person to overcome the danger. If any one of these three ingredients is missing, there is no fear.

In skiing, it is usually the slope which is perceived as the danger, while that which is vulnerable is the skier's body. However, if the skier knows that he is competent enough to ski the trail, there will be no fear. If the skier is incompetent but the hill is too flat to be seen as a danger, there will also be no fear. The third possibility, the skier who does not feel vulnerable to being hurt, is hard to imagine, but theoretically such an individual would also experience no fear.

Fear 1 occurs when illusion governs one or more of these basic components. It increases in proportion to the degree that it exaggerates the danger and vulnerability, or minimizes one's ability to deal with danger. The solution to Fear 1 boils down to simply increasing awareness of the realities in a given situation—that is, increasing awareness of the real danger, of one's true competence and of one's actual vulnerability.

Dispelling Illusionary Danger

To dispel an illusion which either amplifies or minimizes danger, we have to learn to look the threat in the face. In tennis, Tim suggests overcoming the "uh-oh" experience by focusing on the ball's seams. When concentrating on them, the mind sees the ball, not an "uh-oh." As a result, the body doesn't overtighten, sees the ball more as it really is, simply hits it and avoids the error.

Similarly, our greatest obstacle to increasing our awareness of danger in skiing is that we usually resist looking closely at what frightens us. The boy afraid of the boogeyman pulled his covers over his head, making it impossible for him to reject his illusion and easier for his imagination to run wild. Because we don't like to examine danger, it remains an unknown, and the unknown is always more scary. If we hope to overcome the illusions Self 1 projects, we must be willing to look openly at danger and assess its characteristics without resistance.

A good example of using awareness to decrease fear occurred in a lesson I gave to a strong intermediate skier named John, who felt that moguls were his nemesis. He wanted to overcome this fear —especially of the moguls on a run called Big Bumps. However, when we reached the top of the run, John took one look down the slope and panicked.

"I should know better than to try this," he exclaimed. "I'm scared to death just looking down there, much less trying to ski it." His voice had a finality that seemed to say, "Forget it! Let's try another slope."

"I don't care whether we take this run or not," I said, "but as long as we're here, let's try an experiment. It involves simply looking at the slope; I promise I won't ask you to ski it."

"Okay," John agreed reluctantly. "What do you want me to do?"

"Look at the slope as if you didn't hate it and tell me what you see."

"It's damned steep!" John said immediately. "And I hate moguls. I can't help it! Too many of them have tripped me up."

"Which ones do you hate the most?" I asked.

"Those right there where it's almost straight down." he answered, pointing to the steepest part of the slope."

"Take your ski pole," I suggested, "and use it as a plumb line to estimate the angle of that part of the trail. Be as accurate as you can. How many degrees off the horizontal is it?"

After a pause, John looked up surprised, his pole still dangling from his hand at no more than a 20-degree slope.

"It looked more like eighty!" he said sheepishly.

"Now let your eyes look for other steep places, and for the most treacherous moguls. Notice each one carefully and rank them in the order of degree of difficulty."

John started to scrutinize the hillside, pointing out with relish the most difficult spots and telling me in detail what was so hard about them. After a few minutes he said, "Hey, I'm getting to know this mountain pretty well. I might become the world's greatest authority on Big Bumps some-day."

"If you were going to ski this slope—and I'm not suggesting that you actually try it—where would you make your first turn?" I asked.

John looked it over and said, "Okay, I could make my first turn right there. Yeah. I could do that."

"And your second?"

"Yeah. Number two right there, and then there's ... three ... four ... five ..." His voice was calm as he concentrated on his imaginary run. Suddenly he turned to me with a smile and, without another word, pushed his poles into the snow and skied off.

Surprised at the suddenness of his decision, I followed, and was astonished at how much more relaxed and yet aggressive his skiing looked. He was off balance over a couple of moguls, but never really lost control.

At the bottom John was aglow. "Hey, that was fun!" he said. "I loved it. I might even get to like moguls!"

I knew that John felt good about making the run without falling, but I also recognized in his expression the greater sense of achievement which comes from having triumphed over fear.

John's victory was achieved by looking at the mogul field in detail and one at a time. This objective observation shrank the imagined danger and, at the same time, made him aware of the realities of the situation: they were big moguls, but they were ones he could negotiate when unencumbered by fear. Just as in watching the seams of a tennis ball, the mind becomes calmer when it focuses on actual details, the smaller the better.

Speedophobia

Many skiers experience Fear 1 in direct proportion to the speed at which they are moving. Because often they have fallen when going fast, it is easy for them to associate speed with falling. They come to fear speed per se, whether or not they are actually out of control. In short, the rational fear of diminished control can easily turn into an illusion-based fear of speed itself. How to overcome this illusion? In the same way that John overcame his fear of moguls: by increasing one's awareness of speed. This can be a very simple process.

When we ski, we are usually so conscious of trying to either increase or decrease speed that our perception of it is easily distorted. If we want to increase our awareness of speed, we can simply train ourselves to distinguish between its different levels, and to notice the relationship between these speeds and our control.

One way of doing this is to assign the number 5 to what appears to be your maximum speed and zero to standing still. Then as you ski, say aloud the numbers which you believe correspond to the speed at which you are traveling. As most people increase their awareness of these different speeds, they usually find that soon they are skiing comfortably even when moving at a rate which previously had seemed to threaten their control.

It should be noted that discrimination is necessary here. In other words, the speed which may be comfortable in easy conditions can cause you to lose control on more difficult terrain; moreover, it's virtually impossible to be aware of actual speed when you are far out of control. It is the relationship between these three factors—speed, terrain and control—which is crucial.

Looking Out for Ice

One day during an Inner Skiing clinic, Tim fell while taking a lesson from Junior Bounous, the ski-school director at Snow Bird. When he had recovered, Junior asked him, "Do you know why you fell?"

"I have no idea," Tim replied. "Suddenly I just felt off balance, and down I went."

"Look over there," Junior said, pointing to a patch of snow glistening in the sunlight. The difference was barely distinguishable from the packed snow around it. "That's ice. You fell on that."

"Oh," said Tim. "I didn't notice it. I guess I'd better avoid that stuff."

"If you know how it affects your skis," said Junior, "you won't have to avoid it. Ice is more slippery than snow, so when your skis hit an ice patch, they tend to slide faster. Wanting to resist that downward slide, the skier usually leans uphill. Then his skis slide down further, and he ends up in the snow. But if, when your skis hit the ice . . ."

"Yes, if I'd gone with the slide instead of resisting it . . ."

"Right. Now let's go look for some more ice," said Junior.

Tim began looking forward to the challenge of skiing an icy section. What at first had seemed an obstacle to be avoided turned into something to be sought after, experienced and enjoyed. Fear was decreased by curiosity, which led to increased

87

awareness, which in turn reduced the unexpectedness of ice, thereby diminishing its danger. Soon Tim was skiing on ice with a remarkable degree of control.

Other Skiers

Sometimes the most dangerous hazard on a slope is above rather than below you—that is, other skiers. Falling down is frightening enough; being knocked down seems unfair. Again, increased awareness is our best safeguard. Before skiing a trail, notice the density of traffic on it, taking time to become aware of the degree of proficiency of the skiers and being especially alert to the presence of daredevils. Once in motion, we can develop an increased peripheral awareness of nearby skiers, just as players on a team learn to develop peripheral awareness of where their teammates and the opposition are.

What is recommended is *awareness,* not paranoia. If you submit to the fear of collision, you increase your chances of being hit, or at least of falling unnecessarily. If you become distracted by other skiers, who probably wouldn't have hit you in any case, you won't see moguls or subtle changes in the snow. In addition, you yourself become the danger you are trying to avoid. Although in rare circumstances a collision may be unavoidable, the way to minimize the possibility is the same as overcoming irrational fear of it: be aware and trust Self 2.

In summary, the illusionary aspect of a skier's fear of a danger can be decreased and even banished by increasing awareness of the slope itself. To do this, we must learn to overcome our tendencies to avoid looking at what we fear. We need to be willing to know the mogul, the ice, the speed and the other skiers on the slope. This increased knowledge results in increased predictability, increased competence, and, consequently, decreased fear based on illusion.

If you find yourself experiencing Fear 1, allow yourself to look directly at those sights which seem frightening. Let yourself soak in all the details, one by one, of each obstacle. Look the dangers in the eye until you feel you know them—or at least until you feel you want to get to know them better. When you start to see obstacles as welcome challenges, fear will disappear. If you still believe that the slope is too difficult for you to ski safely after you have let yourself really examine it, then look for a somewhat lesser challenge. That's not cowardice but good sense. Remember that it's also possible to be deluded by Fear 1 into minimizing danger.

Fearlessly Foolish

We have all seen the Boomer, who comes down the slopes out of control. He has that look of mad determination on his face as he shoots down the hill, usually without turning at all, his body and face tense. Most of the time, he is wildly off balance, looking as if he's about to crash. Skiing beyond speeds within his control, he endangers not only himself but the skiers around him.

Boomer seems to have no fear, but he also has little discrimination. The opposite of Fearful Fred, he looks through the end of the telescope which reduces the danger of the mountain. Rather than having a low self-image, he has an inflated one, thinking that he can ski anything. As a result, it is impossible for him to discriminate whether a slope is beyond his capabilities or within them.

With bravado, the Boomers of life charge ahead into any situation. Trying to prove to friends that they are unafraid, they take foolish risks. Often they are attempting to cover self-doubt with a façade of fearlessness. In other cases, the Boomer is motivated by boredom with life and seeks situations of meaningless excitement to make it interesting.

Actual Dangers

Of course, there are real dangers to fear in the world, just as there are some slopes which in certain conditions are too steep for even the best skiers. One of the greatest problems Fear 1 presents is that in distracting us with unreal dangers, it prevents us from perceiving the real and present ones. With the world on the verge of a nuclear war, there would still be ski buffs worried about proper form on their turns.

A friend of mine returned from Hawaii amazed by the people of one town who lived on the side of a volcano which frequently smoked and rumbled but hadn't actually erupted for fifty years.

"They were just like us," he told me, "more concerned with the opinion of their neighbors than with the threat of the destruction of their town."

It is as important that we perceive real dangers as they are as it is that we see through illusionary ones. Accurate perception of peril prepares us to cope with it. Still, I have observed that in general people are more likely to indulge in Fear 1 when the actual danger is minimal. My mother was apt to panic if one of her children didn't arrive home when expected. Fantasies of an automobile accident would plague her, she would work herself up into a pronounced state of fear, and would try to alarm the rest of the family. On the other hand, when she found herself in an actual emergency, Mother was the calmest of us all; she knew exactly what to do and would take appropriate action quickly and with full mental presence. Fear 2 had replaced illusion-ridden Fear 1.

Distinguishing between Fear 1 and Fear 2

One may ask, "How do I know when the danger is real and I am feeling Fear 2 or when the danger is that of Self 1 and is simply in my mind?"

If you are in a state of physical and mental preparation (Fear 2), you probably won't even have to ask yourself this question, but if you do find yourself wondering, the best way to discern between the two fears is to notice your body's reactions. Though Fear 1 is born in the imagination, its physical symptoms have a strong sense of reality about them. We are definitely aware of the anxiety churning in the stomach, the shaking of the knees, the dryness in the mouth and the shortness of breath. These physiological responses are no less real for being based on a magnification of danger.

It is simple to tell the difference between the tension and tightness of muscles caused by Fear 1 and the heart-pumping adrenaline rush of Fear 2. In Fear 2 there is a clarity of mind and an intensity of perceptions, while Fear 1 produces panic and unclear vision. Influenced by Fear 1, we usually are afraid to look at the trail closely because it evokes a higher anxiety, whereas Fear 2 enables us to see danger with a heightened sense of detail.

In most cases we experience a mixture of Fear 1 and Fear 2. There is usually some degree of danger present, along with the illusions based on Self 1's imagination. The goal is to decrease or eliminate the *illusionary* component of our fear. To the extent that we succeed, the Fear 2 that remains will increase our physical and psychological ability to meet the challenge at hand.

Awareness of Our Abilities

Once we can see the slope clearly, facing but not exaggerating its perils, the next step is to evaluate our competence to cope with the situation. It is this balance between the degree of difficulty and one's competence which determines the actual danger level of the slope.

We estimate our competence in several ways. The easiest way is through experience. Have we ever before skied a run this steep, this narrow, with moguls and ice? If not, how big a jump is this challenge beyond what we've handled before?

As we take our past experience into consideration, it's a good idea not to forget the specifics of the present situation. A run which might be manageable in the morning when you are most alert and fresh might be quite a different proposition at the end of a tiring day. Also, the trail that in the morning was cushioned with two inches of powder may by afternoon have hardened into crusty patches of ice which would make it a challenge even for skiers more advanced than you. If we trust Self 2, we don't have to think about such factors; we know intuitively. Self 2 knows what it can do. If it is given the chance to really see the slope, it will be able to assess whether the particular challenge is within its capabilities.

I usually trust the intuition of Self 2 in combination with objective observation and memory. I don't trust my thoughts—all those voices in my head that tell me, No, you can't handle that, or Don't be a coward—any dope could make it down there. Instead I ask my intuition, Do you really want to ski this or not? I don't try to persuade myself. I'm open to either answer. If I'm not sure, I look more closely at the hill and ask again, Is this a challenge I'm ready for, or am I taking a foolish risk?

Foolish Risks versus Helpful Challenges

From our experiences, we gradually learn what we can and cannot do. If we never accept challenges, we are left in the dark about all but our most superficial resources. But when our minds are freed from distorted concepts of our ability which are induced by fear, we can accept reasonable challenges without undue risk.

Self 2 knows the next step in one's progress as a skier. Self 1, on the other hand, asks, What will the others think of me if I don't take this run with them? If I can't keep up with them, they'll think I'm scared and won't want to ski with me any more. Or, Wait till I tell everyone I skied this run! Will they be impressed!

Self 1's urgings are related to the maintenance or aggrandizement of its image. Self 2's promptings come from our core and guide us gently toward realizing more of our potential. They seldom push us into an action; instead they lead us quietly, respecting our freedom to accept or postpone a given challenge.

I remember an occasion when Self 1 led me to take a very foolish risk. I was skiing with friends who were more advanced than I was, and they decided to venture through the woods into an unpatrolled area on the back face of the mountain. Something inside me told me that it was not a good idea. I didn't experience the usual symptoms of fear; I felt only a deep conviction that it was wrong for me. I was about to stop and tell my friends that I didn't want to ski this run when Self 1's voice chimed in, If you chicken out, they won't respect you or ski with you any more.

I wavered for a few minutes between that sense of knowing that I was making a mistake and Self 1's blackmail. When we reached the top of the back face, I decided that my first instincts were right. The slope was extremely steep with deep, heavy snow, and there were quite a few trees. But Self 1 came on stronger: You can't quit now! What will they think of you? Giving in to such urgings, I started off. It was a wild run, with many nasty falls—a thoroughly unpleasant experience—and at the end I counted myself lucky not to have been hurt.

Three days later I read in a newspaper that there had been an avalanche on this same slope and that three people had been killed.

Dispelling Illusion about Our Vulnerability

Though the most obvious vulnerability in skiing is the possibility of falling and suffering injury, most skiers are afraid of more than simply hurting their bodies. It is important to recognize that the fear of bruising one's ego, of damaging one's self-image by *failing*, is just as real. Recently when I asked a class of novices how many of them were experiencing fear, eight out of the twelve raised their hands. "Of those who are afraid, is your fear about falling or is it about making a fool of yourself?" I asked. Six of the eight admitted that they were as afraid of failing as they were of falling.

Another kind of fear comes from a less recognized vulnerability. It is what we might call "fear of flying": the fear of going beyond one's expectations, of letting go and relinquishing one's control to Self 2.

Fear of Falling, Failing and Flying

The three kinds of fear—of falling, failing and flying—stem from different vulnerabilities, and in order to overcome their negative effects it is useful to learn to distinguish between them.

Below is a partial list of fears mentioned by participants in a recent ski clinic, categorized by their particular vulnerability.

Fear of Falling

—I'm afraid of going too fast, of not being able to stop, of falling and hurting myself.

—I'm afraid of reinjuring my bad knee.

—Skiing is dangerous, and I'm afraid that if I get hurt I won't be able to go back to work. Even worse, I won't be able to ski again for a long time.

—I hate falling and getting cold and wet.

Fear of Failing

—I'm afraid I'll never learn to ski.

—If I give it everything I've got, and still don't do well, I'll know that I'm really no good. But if I hold back a little, I'll always have the excuse that I wasn't really trying hard.

—I am afraid everyone will see how awkward and uncoordinated I am.

—I don't think I look very good in these ski pants.

—I'm afraid of being embarrassed.

Fear of Flying

—I'm afraid of skiing too well because my friends will think I'm a show-off.

—I'm afraid of letting go of control over myself,

even though I skied much better the few times I tried it.

—It's frightening to ski really well because then you have a reputation to live up to.

—When I really let go, it's as if part of me dies.

An effective way of increasing your awareness of vulnerability in general is to ask yourself some questions. What possible harm can come to me? Does the harm I fear threaten my body or my ego? Then be as specific as you can.

If you realize you're afraid of falling, don't stop there. Ask yourself what is likely to happen if you fall. In the particular situation, do you really think it is possible, to hurt yourself seriously? Even if the answer is yes, what then? Is it the pain, the incapacitation or the expense you fear? On the other hand, if you are only afraid that falling will make you cold and wet, follow that to its full conclusion as well. In short, neither exaggerate nor minimize the consequences of falling, failing or flying.

I once asked a frightened skier what was the worst she imagined could happen. She answered that she wasn't as afraid of hurting herself as of not skiing as well as her friends.

"What would happen then?"

"Well, they might like me less, and not ask me to go skiing with them."

"Okay. And then?"

"Well, I might lose them as friends."

"And after that?"

"I guess I'd feel lonely . . . No, I'm sure I'd find more friends."

"And then?"

"They might even be better friends than the ones who would like me only if I skied well."

With little help from me, she had seen through her exaggerated vulnerability, and now her fear was gone.

Fear of Falling

Of course, the human body is vulnerable to injury when moving too fast to be able to control itself. We have discussed increasing one's awareness of the actual danger from the hill or from other skiers. Now let us examine how to increase awareness of one's vulnerability to being physically hurt.

Some people are more prone to injury than others, and so they experience more fear. For example, a ten-year-old girl in perfect health, with a little extra padding where it counts, is not as vulnerable as an older woman who has recently torn a ligament in her leg. If for some reason your body is particularly fragile because of a recent injury or some other structual weakness, it doesn't make sense to ski beyond your safety zone.

To think that you can't be hurt would be silly, but it's equally irrational—and more common— to exaggerate the probabilities of injury if you fall. Realism is gained by paying attention to experience—your own and that of others.

When you fall, try to notice what happens. There's no need to fall on purpose, but when and if you do fall, you can learn something from it. If you fall as a result of going too fast and allow yourself to experience the pain, you will probably be less inclined to go out of control the next time. If you find the fall didn't hurt as much as you thought it would, you learn that not all falls are painful, and your fear will decrease. This is often the case with beginners, who generally dread falling, and this usually causes them to tighten and sit back. But when they do fall, they find that it wasn't as bad as they had imagined. With their fear lessened, they relax more and hence fall less. I saw an example of this at exactly the opposite end of the spectrum—that is, the experts—while watching on television a special downhill race without turns designed to break speed records. To cut down resistance from the wind and snow, the racers used special equipment and reached speeds of up to 120 mph. On one of the runs a racer had a spectacular crash but was unharmed. In an interview afterward the skier said that the fall had actually made him more relaxed. Prior to the run he had been afraid of what might happen, and so was tight. After falling he realized that the worst wasn't so bad, and so wasn't as afraid on his next run.

In other words, whether novice or expert, it is important to learn by example; otherwise, experience has a habit of repeating itself until the inherent lesson is learned.

I once gave a ski lesson to a beginner, Charles, an Englishman who had been reading *The Inner Game of Tennis* and was enthusiastic about its approach. Whenever he fell, he would laugh and exclaim, "Nothing is good or bad. Falling is fine. Falling is fun!"

As I watched Charles I noticed that he seemed to fall whenever he was even slightly off balance. It was a cold day, and I grew tired of helping him put his skis back on every time he took a tumble. Finally, when he was sprawled out in the snow again, still blissfully smiling, I asked, "Tell me, how is it down there? Are you cold? How long does it take us to get your skis back on each time?"

Charles paused, assessed his body and his situation, and then said, "Actually, it's damned cold down here, and I'd rather be skiing than doing up my bindings all the time." Thereafter, he fell less.

Falling is falling—nothing more, nothing less. If it were more fun to fall than to stand up, few children would learn to walk. Falling is supposed to be a little uncomfortable; why pretend the discomfort isn't there? Painful falls teach us not to take unnecessary risks, define the extent of our vulnerability and help us to make more intelligent choices.

Many skiers are more afraid of pain than of injury. The pain of a fall is real, but fear exaggerates it, often making it seem more intense than it actually is. Pain needs to be experienced as it is in order to avoid distortion. It is the body's way of telling us something; we need to attend to it rather than to ignore or to exaggerate it. Again the principle is the same: experience what is; be aware and learn.

Memories of Past Injuries

In my second winter of skiing, I took a bad fall and tore the ligaments in my right knee. It was quite painful. Even more painful was the ankle-to-groin cast that I had to wear for a month.

After the cast was removed, I exercised religiously until the leg was back to normal. That spring I played lacrosse, a physically demanding game that requires a lot of running, and that summer I was a lifeguard, swimming constantly in the ocean and running on the beach. My knee never bothered me; in fact, I don't believe I even thought about the injury.

But the first time I went skiing that winter a voice in my mind reminded me, "Better be careful. Your knee might not be strong enough, and you don't want to injure it again." I started hesitating a little, tightening up, favoring my right leg so that I wouldn't put all my weight down on it. As a result, I constantly fell when turning to my left.

Memories of past injuries enhance the power of Fear 1, telling us that the worst that has happened is about to happen again. Fear works by association. If we take a bad fall in a particular circumstance, the next time we're in a similar situation we're apt to experience fear. The present may be void of real danger, but the fear will still be there.

Memories are only memories. If we can keep our minds in the present, we will see the situation as it is and know how to respond. But if we let our minds project the past onto the future, we will see ghosts and tighten up, responding to the illusion instead of what is really there, thus increasing the likelihood of another injury.

Overcoming Fear of Failure

People, especially in our Western culture, are greatly concerned about not performing well enough to meet the expectations of self or others.

It is not so much a fear of not accomplishing a given task or of attaining a certain standard, but of having the stigma of failure attached to one's self-image. It is Self 1's fear of losing face.

When I asked a young man who was worried that he would never graduate from a stem to a parallel turn what the worst thing was that could happen to him if he failed to improve, he answered, "Well, I'd never get off the beginners' slope."

"Would that be so bad?"

"Well, no, I don't really mind skiing the bunny trails. What would hurt is thinking that I'm a failure as a skier. I'd lose my self-esteem if I didn't get better."

So many of us have been conditioned for so long to measure our self-worth according to how we perform—especially at sports—that loss of self-esteem on the slopes seems a matter of importance. Identifying ourselves with our performance, we believe that we *are* how we ski. If we ski well, we feel that we are good, deserving of recognition, love and respect. If we fail, we fear that we will lose the love and respect we need.

This belief that one's self-worth can be defined by success is implicit in the minds of many people, and I know of no way to overcome it than by gradually seeing through the myth on which it is based. Human worth is not proportionate to human achievement. It simply cannot be measured in talent, position, age, wealth, roles, belongings and trophies. Why not? Because the value of human life is beyond measure. At his core every person is invaluable and deserves all possible respect and love—not for anything that he or she has achieved, but simply by virtue of being human. The truth of this assertion is not easily acknowledged, but as one grows in self-awareness it will be gradually recognized.

Estelle was a middle-aged psychological counselor. After skiing for one morning, she was in tears and didn't want to continue. "I've simply never been able to learn anything in a group. Ever since high school I've failed at everything I tried to learn with other people around. I've achieved a lot of success, but it has always been with what I've picked up on my own. I really want to learn to ski, but I'm terrified because I know I'm going to fail again."

It was clear that Estelle wanted to realize two separate goals: to learn how to ski, and to overcome her lifelong intimidation in group-learning situations. I asked her which of the two she wanted more, and she answered that what she wanted most was to overcome her fear of failure in groups. "After all, if I wasn't so afraid, I'm sure I could learn to ski, and a lot of other things too."

Once this choice was made, all that was left for Estelle was to look failure in the eye and see just what it consisted of. We discussed in detail the worst that could happen if she failed to learn how to ski. "The last time you failed, where did it hurt? What real difference did it make? Did failing really mean that you were a failure? Who are you, anyway—someone who is worthwhile only when she succeeds, and unlovable when she fails?" Estelle edged closer to a recognition that she was neither her successes nor her failures, but the one person who was experiencing both. When she looked closely at the possibility of failing in the group ski lesson, she realized that it would be only a little embarrassing. She saw that failure was one experience, success another, and that both were simply experiences in the life of the experiencer, herself.

When we parted, Estelle was looking forward to skiing that afternoon. She had no idea whether she would succeed or fail, but somehow that wasn't the most important thing any more. What she *was* sure of was that she could learn and benefit from whatever happened. She was going to be alert and appreciate learning more about what failure or success really was. Already she seemed to be waking from the worst of her nightmare, and the decrease in Fear 1 could only make learning to ski easier.

In almost every case the key to overcoming fear of failure is a process of breaking one's attachment to results. Whenever we convince ourselves that results are all that count, we fall into an anxiety which paradoxically limits our ability to achieve those results. When the tennis player thinks he *has* to get his serve in because it's game point, tension takes over and fluidity and accuracy vanish. The same is true in skiing when we *have* to make a turn. The hardest thing in any achievement-oriented endeavor is to recognize that it is more important to stay fully present and aware than to strain for results. Our maximum potential is a by-product of awareness and of letting Self 2 express itself. Overconcern about achievement causes tightness and restriction of our bodies. The greatest competitors want to win, and hate to lose, but they aren't *afraid* to lose.

What is the value of learning a parallel turn if

we neither enjoy ourselves nor learn something that can improve the quality of our life? Detachment from the god of success frees one from fear of failing, and then success comes much easier, for whatever it is worth.

Only Self 1 is vulnerable to lack of achievement; Self 2 neither benefits from success nor is hurt by failure. Children recognize this: they chant, "Sticks and stones can break my bones, but names can never harm me." The more we are able to recognize that failure is only a name and that we are not our Self 1, the less vulnerable and less fearful of failure we will be. The only real failure is not to recognize that you are more than your Self 1.

Fear of Flying

Self 1's third major vulnerability is its fear of achieving a state beyond its control by becoming totally involved in the present. During such a breakthrough experience, Self 1 becomes so absorbed in what's happening that it stops thinking, fearing, doubting, instructing, congratulating or analyzing. Though this quieting of the mind helps our performance immeasurably because of the resulting increase in awareness, it is a kind of dying for Self 1. After the experience is over, it is always surprised: Wow, I don't believe it! Who was doing that skiing? How did it happen? Self 1 likes such skiing, of course, but not the fact that it occurred without any help from its voice. What would happen if the skier realized he didn't need Self 1—for skiing or anything else?

Self 1 experiences a dilemma whenever we start to perform near the level of our highest expectations. It wants the excellence, but not the loss of self. It is a hard choice, but usually Self 1 chooses its own existence at the cost of excellence. Tim often gives an example from the tennis court of what he calls the three-ball player. "This is the person who, after the ball has gone over the net three times, says nervously to himself, Wow, this is a long rally. Of course, fear ends the rally shortly after the player becomes conscious of how well he is doing."

This same self-consciousness exists in skiers as they begin to surpass their expected levels, and it originates in Self 1's fear of flying. Having surrendered temporarily to Self 2's control and skiing "out of one's mind," Self 1 intrudes itself on the scene and sabotages the breakthrough run. Very few of us can experience a peak performance for long without Self 1's rushing in to admire, congratulate, take credit, or in some other way separating us from the experience. It's as if Self 1 is saying to Self 2, Okay, you've had your fun, but I'm not going to let you run the show any longer.

After the initial amazement and congratulations, Self 1 then generally attempts to repeat the breakthrough experience, but this time under its own control. It starts thinking about how it happened and tries to make it happen again: Gee, I was really skiing out of my head . . . that was beautiful . . . I think I must have really been letting go and being more aggressive . . . I'll just keep being aggressive . . . Okay, bend, weight, unweight, lean into it . . . attack. It isn't the same experience with all those thoughts and all that straining, but at least Self 1 feels comfortable now that the reins are in his hands again. It is programmed to sacrifice the beauty for the known sense of control, the excellent for the familiar.

There is probably nothing so challenging as changing one's means of self-control from Self 1 to Self 2. Learning new skills or new sports, or even learning to move in outer space, is nothing compared with the sense of the unknown when we change our way of controlling our bodies. Nothing is quite so beautiful as Self 2 action, and our dilemma is that we know this; we know it by the breakthrough moments when we left our minds and fell into the natural control of Self 2, the same self that produced the excellence and joys of our early childhood. To suddenly abandon Self 1 requires more courage than most of us have. But it is possible to do it gradually, and the more we come to trust Self 2, the more we lose our fear of flying.

Fear of Fear

Often when a skier is caught in Fear 1 he is so acutely conscious of his terror that it is difficult for him to focus attention on the slope. When the physiological symptoms of fear are overpowering, the skier often begins to be frightened of the fear itself: I know I can never ski a hill like this when I'm so petrified. At times like this, illusion can be decreased by focusing on the symptoms of the fear.

A good example of the power of such awareness occurred during a program Tim and I were giving to a group of three hundred skiers. Wanting to make his point by example, Tim asked how many people would be afraid to come up on stage and face the audience. About a hundred people raised their hands. Then he asked, "Of those who would be afraid to come up, how many would do it anyway, if I requested it?" About two-thirds raised their hands. "Of those who feel they are too terrified to come up here, is there one or two who'd be willing to do it for the sake of an experiment?" Tim asked. One hesitating hand was raised, and Tim encouraged a young, slightly overweight woman to come forward. Once onstage she didn't face the audience, but stood sideways looking toward Tim, who asked her name and how she was feeling. "Barbara, and I'm scared to death!" she replied while blushing and giggling.

"Of what?" Tim asked.

"I don't know—all I know is I'm petrified." She was obviously more conscious of her fear than of the audience.

Tim asked, "How do you know you are afraid?"

Barbara looked surprised. "Because I feel it."

"Where are these feelings located in your body?"

"Well, my heart is pounding and my face is hot, but mostly I can feel my knees trembling."

"Are your knees shaking right now?" Tim asked.

"Yes."

"Does it hurt?"

"No, but I wish they'd calm down a bit."

"If shaking as much as they possibly could were measured as ten and not shaking at all was zero, how much are your knees shaking?"

"About nine," Barbara replied, but by now her voice was considerably more calm.

Tim asked if her heart was still pounding as hard and her face still as hot, then told her to focus her attention on her knees again.

"Huh, they're down to about five," said Barbara with surprise.

"All right," said Tim, "let's see what happens when you look out at the audience."

Barbara turned and stared blankly at the sea of faces. "Wow, the knees just shot back up to ten."

"Just keep looking out there and at the same time pay attention to your knees," Tim suggested.

Soon Barbara's knees were only at four or five, even though she was facing the audience.

"Where is the easiest place to look?" Tim asked.

Barbara stared at the back of the hall and reported that her knees were only at two. Then Tim asked her how far she could bring her eyes toward the front of the hall without an increase in the shaking. Her gaze came forward and stopped near the middle. "I can get about halfway," she said in a voice which indicated that she was becoming absorbed in the experiment.

"What do you see there that makes your knees shake?" Tim asked.

"Some people aren't smiling," Barbara answered, and started to laugh.

"Point to the people who aren't smiling," Tim suggested.

When she did, everyone started to laugh, and Barbara joined in.

"Look at the front four rows."

"Oops," she said. "Back up to a four."

"Look individually at the people in those seats," Tim suggested.

Some of them started to wave at her, and soon

Barbara was laughing again. "I feel great," she said. "My fear is down to almost nothing."

Barbara stayed onstage while Tim continued his discussion of fear. Fear is like pain, he suggested; not something bad in itself, but an indication from the body that something is the matter. Fear 2 indicates that there is a real and present danger and the need for greater alertness, whereas Fear 1 signals the presence of an illusion about some unreal, imagined danger. But it, too, calls for a heightening of awareness—an indication to get out of one's concepts and return to what *is*. When recognized, both fears can be useful barometers.

There were questions from the audience, and finally one about the experiment with Barbara. Tim hesitated, as if thinking how best to answer the question, and then turned and asked Barbara to reply. Much to everybody's surprise, Barbara gave a fluent and articulate answer, with poise, calmness and no hesitation. Without the interference of Fear 1 she had become a different person; in fact, the change was so striking that some people thought the demonstration had been planned in advance. But Barbara knew that it hadn't, and during the next break she came up to tell us that this had been one of the most important experiences of her life.

Awareness can focus on fear without fear. When we identify with fear we are afraid; when we identify with awareness we are that which is looking at the fear. This awareness is the part of us that is always calm, and it can be a helpful refuge when we are under attack by Fear 1.

As long as we identify with the parts of ourselves which change, inevitably we are subject to fear. To gain final freedom Socrates exhorted man to "know thyself." Castaneda's teacher, Don Juan, called those who attain this goal Men of Knowledge, pointing to the final destination of one who plays the Inner Game to win.

5

Improving

For whatever reason they ski—fun, health, a chance to meet people—most skiers are disappointed if they haven't improved after a week on the slopes. The desire to ski faster and with more control on increasingly challenging runs is as natural as it is common.

All God's creatures have the desire to actualize their potential. A bird, for example, is born with the potential to fly, and its progress is simple and continuous. Improvement needs only some time, experience and a little guidance from its parents. Without worrying about whether or not it is becoming more skillful, it manages to learn to soar on currents of air, to dive, turn and glide. The bird's improvement is never in doubt; there is no strain, no forcing, no inferiority complex, no inflated ego —and amazingly enough, no lack of coordination.

Yet among human beings we see all of the above qualities, including lack of coordination, in their efforts to improve. Why is development so easy for the bird, and so difficult and frustrating for people? Why do humans try so hard to improve when improvement is so effortless for the rest of nature?

Fritz Perls, the father of Gestalt therapy, answered this question with the ironic insight that human beings are the only species of life which has the capability of interfering with its own

115

growth. The human being tends to block this natural process by doubting his potential. He believes that if he can't do something right away it's because the potential isn't there. He concludes that improvement means *adding* something which he doesn't already have, *becoming* something which he isn't. "I'm not a good skier," he says to himself, "and to become one I'll have to acquire the necessary skills from somewhere outside of me."

In truth, what he needs to understand is that improvement is the natural process of helping something already inside himself to emerge. The oak exists within the acorn. The bird improving its flying technique is simply manifesting a potential inside itself from birth. To be sure, the acorn needs water, earth and sun, and the bird needs guidance and experience, but the growth of each is a natural development of an already existing potential.

Although the distinction between these two approaches may seem obscure, the difference they make is startlingly clear. Improvement by allowing one's potential to emerge is unstrained, enjoyable and remarkably steady. Improvement by trying to acquire an ability or quality which one assumes isn't there is usually frustrating and often halting. It is only because we employ our unique capability to impede our progress that we find improvement a problem at all, and this is why the road to improvement is often so difficult for the skier.

Two Kinds of Improvement

Because man interferes with his growth, his performance varies a great deal, often falling far below his capabilities. All athletes are confounded by their repeated tendency to perform brilliantly one day, only to fall apart the next. The level of a skier's performance at any given time is the difference between his present capabilities and the extent of Self 1's interference with them. He will ski below his actual ability in direct proportion to the extent of his mental interference. Free of Self 1 limitations, he will ski his best—that is, up to the limits of his potential as it has been developed to date. Further improvement will entail additional experiences to stimulate new growth.

Thus, there are really two kinds of improvement for humans. The first brings a person's skill closer to his present capabilities; the second is to learn new skills.

The remainder of this chapter will discuss the first kind of improvement: the ways of recognizing and overcoming the major obstacles that prevent us from skiing as well as we already can. The next chapter will discuss ways to facilitate the process of developing new skills.

Letting What's Inside Come Out

In their desire to improve faster, many skiers overlook or neglect entirely the first kind of improvement. They think that they aren't progressing fast enough if they aren't learning or practicing something new. But this is not necessarily true; the mental interference that is keeping you from skiing your best right now will also make it more difficult to acquire new skills. Before replacing the dim light bulb in your dusty attic, it makes sense to clean the bulb first to see how much light it gives off with the dust removed. Similarly, in skiing it makes sense to first clear away the doubts and fears of Self 1 which prevent you from shining your brightest.

Let's take the example of a skier who thinks of himself as awkward, and who has relatively little self-confidence in his ability. Because Self 1's beliefs affect one's actions, the skier's lack of confidence will be reflected in his performance. For instance, he may lean uphill, not bend his knees, and plant his poles stiffly and with bad timing because he is gripping them too tightly. If he sets out to correct each of these problems, it is apt to take him the better part of a season before these manifestations of his poor self-image are corrected. If he tries to change everything at once, his mind will become overloaded with multiple instructions and skiing becomes even more awkward. Yet if he takes each correction one at a time, he runs into other problems. If he decides to begin by leaning forward more, he is fearful because of lack of confidence, and so he has to force himself. This strain causes tightness and awkwardness. Even if he succeeds in making his body lean forward, his jaw is probably clenched with tension and his shoulders are even tighter than usual. In fact, he may even invent new postures to express his self-doubt. Trying to get the body to do what the mind doesn't want it to do is usually frustrating and time-consuming.

On the other hand, if the same skier is helped to overcome some of his self-doubt the errors that it is causing will begin to disappear spontaneously. Feeling more confident, he will find it easier to lean forward and to weight his outside ski in the turn; his shoulders, arms and knees will be more relaxed and his pole plants will improve automatically. Eliminating only a single mental obstacle produces many physical improvements. As a result, the skier gains confidence in his ability, which in turn reduces resistance to absorbing new skills. Indeed, the skier may discover that what he thought was a new skill was already within his present capacity.

Self-Image as an Obstacle

Probably the greatest obstacles to growth of all kinds are our concepts about ourselves. By believing that I am not good at the sport, I limit how well I will let myself ski. Believing that I can't make good parallel turns, I usually won't. Nursing the idea that I am an intermediate skier, I delay the process of becoming an advanced one. These

119

beliefs about ourselves are like the programs fed into a computer which, though it has the capacity to do many complicated tasks, can only perform within the limits of its program.

Self 2 is like an extremely sophisticated computer which receives an incredible amount of data from its experience, stores it in memory banks, and then uses it to refine movement and develop new skills. If you have a computer with the capacity to solve every conceivable square root, but program it only for numbers up to 100, it will not give you the answer if you ask for the square root of 1938. The limited programming doesn't cancel the computer's memory or mean that it lacks the capability; it simply prevents the use of its full potential.

Self 1 limits Self 2 in the same way. Its negative beliefs can't decrease Self 2's potential, but it can and does restrict its realization. Self 1 can't prevent Self 2 from being able to make a parallel turn if that skill is already within its capabilities, but it can keep the parallel turn from happening. Likewise, if Self 2 is continually being fed the idea that it is uncoordinated, to the extent that that programming is accepted, coordination is sabotaged. It is this tendency of Self 1 to impose limiting concepts on Self 2 that is the fundamental means by which man interferes with his own growth.

This is not to say that if you tell your Self 2 that it can ski expertly that it will allow you to do so. You can't program a computer to solve calculus problems simply by telling it that it is a great mathematician. This is the principal flaw of so-called "positive thinking." Self 2 cannot accomplish tasks simply because you repeatedly tell it that it can; it will do so only with growth and experience, and when it has the necessary sensory data in its memory bank. Human computers can be programmed with positive or negative concepts, but neither of these alters Self 2's actual capacity. Telling yourself that you are an advanced skier when in fact you are a beginner is not going to make you an expert, and may even be dangerous. Rather than feeding in positive programs —which you may not even believe in—to replace negative ones—which you probably do—it is more effective to focus on eliminating any limiting concepts. It is extraordinary to see just how much a self-concept can interfere with one's ability to ski, and how much improvement will take place immediately after its removal.

Harriet Lets It Happen

I remember vividly an episode involving a woman in her late thirties named Harriet who joined one of my intermediate classes. Riding up in the chair, she complained of having been an intermediate skier for eight years; she was hoping that perhaps an Inner Skiing class could get her out of this rut.

My first impression of Harriet was of a woman who tried to please. She wore her make-up and clothes with an almost overconscientious attention to detail. Her voice was cheerful but almost inaudible and her language was as precise as her graying bangs. When she took her first run, I saw that her skiing fit her personality: she looked good and had no major flaws, but she was overly careful. Her turns were executed with a technique that reflected many hours of lessons conscientiously

121

practiced, but they lacked rhythm, fluidity and aggressiveness. Her movements looked deliberate and controlled, and she didn't allow herself to pick up the speed that the level of her technique seemed able to handle.

At the end of her first run Harriet shook her head self-critically, and I asked, "What's the matter?"

"Well, to tell you the truth, I don't know. I know that my form is okay. It should be. I've worked at it enough. But I'm really not satisfied. I'd like to be able to take more advanced runs, but I don't feel I'm good enough yet. I sometimes think I'm going to be an intermediate skier forever."

At this moment I used an Inner Game trick which often helps a student shed a limiting self-image. "Harriet, what kind of skiing would satisfy you?" I asked. "Can you give me an idea of how good you would really like to be?"

"Well, I think I'd like—"

"No, not in words. Show me," I interrupted. "Give me a visual image of what you want. Right now. Don't even think about it—just do it."

Harriet took off, skiing thirty yards down the intermediate slope in a manner very different from the way she handled her first run. A lot of her careful control disappeared, and in its place there was more spontaneity and power.

"Was that a little more how you'd like to be able to ski?" I asked when I joined her.

"Yes, something like that. I can't put my finger on what I was doing differently, but it certainly felt different. That was fun," she said excitedly.

"Your skiing looked more aggressive to me," I said noncommittally.

"Oh," she said, looking embarrassed. "Well,

maybe, but I'm really not the aggressive type."

"Would you be willing to show me how you'd ski if you were?"

Harriet hesitated a moment and then skied downhill another fifty yards, amazing me and the rest of the class. Instead of taking her usual long traverses between turns she headed directly down the fall line, linking short crisp turns and picking up speed; she was attacking the slope, driving her knees and edging sharply. To be sure, she lost a measure of refinement as she poled vigorously and leaned forward, abandoning all caution, but considering the degree of difficulty of the terrain her skiing showed remarkable improvement.

"Is that what aggressive skiing would be?" I asked.

"I didn't think I had that in me," she exclaimed, apparently overwhelmed by the experience. "I loved it, but I doubt if I could keep it up. It's really not like me."

I could see that Harriet was confronting a common Inner Game dilemma. Should she believe the image she held of herself or what she had just experienced? Could this single example of aggressiveness replace a whole lifetime of trying to please others? "Can I be aggressive in the future? Why haven't I let myself ski this way before?" she might have wondered. It was not an easy choice to make: the safety of her old, carefully circumscribed self-image against the risk of her expanded sense of self. She had to choose between improvement and shedding a self-image.

What stunned the group was how improved Harriet's skiing had become almost instantly. She hadn't been given a single technical instruction, yet technical changes in her skiing occurred along with greater fluidity and rhythm. It was obvious that the ability to ski so well had been inside Harriet the whole time. What had released her potential was that she had ignored—perhaps only temporarily—the self-image that had been restricting her. In thinking of herself as unaggressive, she had skied unaggressively; but since she had never programmed herself to think that she couldn't "show" someone what aggressive skiing was like, she was able to do it, and skied much closer to her.

The next day Harriet reported triumphantly that for the first time in her life she had skied an advanced run, a challenge that had been within her technical competence for a long time, and had enjoyed it enormously.

What are the beliefs that you have about your skiing? Some of the more common ones are: "I'm not well coordinated"; "I'm not aggressive enough"; "I can't ski the fall line, take moguls, make parallel turns"; "I am a beginner." Now think for a moment. Have you ever had an experience which refutes that belief? If you are like most skiers I've known, you've had a run, or at least a few turns, in which your performance contradicted your self-image.

Do you believe your experience—which has shown you that you are capable of more—or your self-image? One way of resolving the contradiction is to chalk off the good experience to luck or fate or newly sharpened edges. This prevents you from setting yourself up for disappointment and frustration, but it also keeps you from improving. The frightening alternative is to realize that there is more potential inside you than you ever realized, and that the real challenge is to shed whatever is keeping your potential from developing.

How Self-Images Are Formed

The tendency to form constricting self-concepts is so common that most of the time we don't even know we are doing it. The process can start innocently enough by identifying with our performance. Take John, who is eager to ski well and is about to take his first run of the day. In the past he has had both good days and bad, but being uncertain of himself, he's anxious about what will happen today. If his first few turns are a bit awkward, he may say to himself, This looks like a bad run. Sure enough, it is, and by the time he reaches the bottom he has convinced himself that the whole day will be a washout. After another run he notices that he is rotating his upper body as he turns—an error he'd thought he'd corrected last season; now he thinks, "I have lousy form. I hope no one's watching me." A few discouraging falls later, his dominant thought is, I can't ski moguls to save my life. Finally in despair, he reaches the conclusion that he is a bad skier and that he ought to give up the sport.

In the matter of minutes, John has increasingly defined and limited himself by his beliefs that (1) he is going to have a bad run and a bad day; (2) he has lousy form; (3) he can't ski moguls; and (4) he will never be a good skier.

After programming himself for a day of poor skiing, John has begun a process which progressively programs a poor self-image. By thinking that he has bad form he identifies with a *possession*—his form. By using the word "can't," he limits his potential. "Can" and "can't" are among the most powerful words we use to define ourselves. His most limiting concepts are those thoughts that start with "I am" and "I am not." Once he believes he is a bad skier, he won't allow himself to have good form, be able to ski moguls or be the skier he potentially is.

Self 1's image forming can go so far as to shape one's very sense of identity. At the end of a few days of unsatisfactory skiing, he may conclude that not only is he a bad skier but he is uncoordinated in general. After a few frustrating days back at the office he may extend the program to include all activities, and tell himself that he is incompetent. From there it is only a short step to "I'm no good at all."

How could John have stopped himself from forming these negative self-concepts? Not by trying to generate a positive self-image, but by forming no *self-image at all*. Having made three awkward turns, he could simply have observed to himself, Hey, those turns felt pretty awkward; this would have been simply an accurate description of a past event. When he fell on a mogul, if he had thought, Well, I haven't skied a mogul well yet today, instead of believing that he couldn't ski them at all, he would leave open, and perhaps even encourage, the possibility of improvement.

Does John gain anything by believing he's going to have a bad day and that he's an inferior skier? He gains a sense of security by predicting what is going to happen, thus preventing possible disappointment. At least at the end of the day he can say, "Well, I knew I wasn't going to have a good day." Or if someone sees him fall, he defends himself against embarrassment by thinking, Yeah, I know I'm lousy—so what? At the expense of improvement he gains a sense of comforting predictability about the future and about himself.

John's mistake is shared by many of us in our culture: we tend to identify ourselves with how we perform. If I ski badly I tend to feel badly about myself and to believe that I am less worthy of respect. On the other hand, if I ski well I feel good about myself, and therefore am convinced that I myself am worthy of respect and approval. I try to prove myself by improving my skiing. Self 1's concern with establishing a worthwhile identity for itself leads most of us into "the proving game." Being an exercise which focuses wholly on self-image, it distracts us from and inhibits our natural process of improvement.

The Proving Game

An observant woman, Lynne Kaufman, who attended a five-day Inner Game residential workshop described in an article for *California Living* the importance the proving game has for some players:

> I find my way to condominium, Pelican 19, in time for lunch; the large living room is furnished with six round tables, the curtains drawn to an expensive view of sandpipers, cormorants and gulls. The other twenty workshop members straggle in. . . . most in their thirties and forties. Californians, fit,

tan, professionals. Some verbal sparring at lunch; who are you, what do you do, who do you know, where have you been? Soon we will all be undergoing the tennis player's acid test—"Want to hit some?" and within ten strokes we will each have the definitive answer to life's supreme question— HOW GOOD ARE YOU?

Tim described his early involvement with the proving game when he was a ten-year-old tennis player. "I used to get up at six-forty-five on a summer morning, dress, make and eat breakfast (scrambled eggs and fried hot dogs) in six minutes flat, run a mile and a half down a hill to the Pebble Beach gatehouse, and then either hitchhike or run the remaining three miles to the tennis courts. Arriving at least an hour before anyone else, I would practice forehands and backhands against the green wooden backboard, 1041, 1042, 1043, 1044, etc., ad nauseam.

"When players finally arrived, I would play with anyone who was willing, not leaving until dark after at least twelve or fifteen sets, a lot of drilling under my belt and half an inch of rubber worn off my tennis shoes. If you asked me why was I practicing so hard, or whether I was having fun, I probably would have been surprised. Sure, it was fun when I was playing well, but I wasn't doing it for fun. I was doing it to get good. I didn't know why it was so important for me to get good. It took thirty years for me to find out that the 'good' I was trying to 'get' I already was."

For most people the proving game starts with a definite but often unrecognized sense of "not being good enough the way I am." The basic idea of the game is to earn respect and admiration from yourself and others by learning to do something

128

well. "I may be homely, but I'll show them! Wait till they see how many A's I get. That will prove my worth." Or, "They all think I'm just an uncoordinated brain. I'll take up skiing, practice hard and become a really good skier. Then they'll accept me."

The essential point about the proving game is that it is usually played to substantiate something that in our heart we doubt is true. Fred sets out to ski more aggressively, takes more risks and becomes a macho skier in order to prove that he's a "real man"—which he must doubt if he has to verify it. In general, players of the proving game tend to doubt their intrinsic self-worth, and spend their lives trying to demonstrate the opposite of their basic self-image.

The Weaknesses of the Proving Game

Trying Too Hard

Provers always strain because the proving game begins in self-doubt, and trying is precisely the kind of effort which results from doubt. When a skier believes that he can make a parallel turn, he doesn't try, he just does it. We don't try to sit down; we simply do so. Trying is the overcompensation of a mind that doubts you can do something, and it almost invariably leads to the tightening of too many muscles, the most common single cause of error in sport. It takes effort to ski down a slope and make turns, but it doesn't take trying.

Trying employs unnecessary muscles (we might call them "trying muscles") which inevitably restrict fluidity and cause a tension and awkwardness that hinder our performance. A well-known track coach says that tight fists and a clenched jaw are the sure signs of a slow time. He gets the best results from his athletes by asking them to run at four-fifths speed instead of all-out.

"Not trying" requires a trust in Self 2's potential, the essential ingredient missing from the proving game.

Here Comes the Judge

The proving game necessarily involves the selection of one or more judges who will approve or disapprove of me and my skiing. Often we end up paying more attention to them than to our performance on the mountain, thereby losing touch with the subtle feedback necessary to improve. As a result, my skiing plateaus and the approval I seek becomes more difficult to achieve.

Most players of the proving game start out seeking only the approval of their parents, but soon the list includes friends, teachers, coaches and almost everyone on the slope. The more people I let sit in judgment over me, the more I have to live up to conflicting standards of right and wrong. When I give authority to others to judge my worth, I am at their mercy—much like the gladiators whose very lives depended upon the whim of the emperor.

Frequently the most merciless of emperors is my own Self 1, whose favorite role is to sit in judgment over me and everything I do. Who gives me the authority to judge even myself?

No Win

Trying to win the proving game is an endless endeavor. As one goal is reached another presents itself. First I had to make my highschool swimming team, but the status of my varsity jacket wore out before the jacket did, so I had to earn a city championship trophy. Even a mantle covered with trophies, plus making all-American, didn't satisfy me for long, or prove what I wanted to. Doing well only led me deeper and deeper into the game. I doubted whether even the national championships or the Olympics would do it. Perhaps the answer lay in proving myself in a career— seeing how much money I could make—in the way I dressed or the company I kept and so forth. But the game was never-ending; there was always further to go to reach the top of one ladder, and then I was confronted with any number of other ladders to climb.

A basic law of nature is that the exterior is a reflection of the interior, and this is the primary reason that it is impossible to ever really win the proving game. We can't better ourselves by polishing our exterior image.

Because the proving game is founded on a false premise that "I am my performance," the only way to win the game is to stop playing it. How can you do so? First, by recognizing that you are playing it, and then by realizing that it is not the game you want to play. You begin to question yourself: Why is my image so important? Why do I feel badly about myself when I ski poorly, and glow when someone tells me that they think I'm terrific at it? Does my satisfaction come from believing that I'm a good skier and being recognized as such by others, or does it come from actually skiing well?

These two satisfactions are quite different. The first is Self 1's taking pleasure in a self-image and leads us into the proving game. The second comes from experience, and guides us toward the discovery game, in which the skier seeks to experience his potential rather than to prove it.

The Discovery Game

In skiing this simply means exploring one's already existing potential to improve. Instead of trying to confirm something about myself by the way I ski, or to predict how I'm going to ski my next run, I let go of expectations and concepts and see what happens. My aim is to experience my skiing fully, to be as conscious as possible of body movement, skis, snow, rhythm and balance. If I have a breakthrough run, I enjoy it, but I neither expect that I will ski that well on the next run, nor that I won't. Similarly, if I have a run which I know is less than my best, I don't form a judgment about myself or my skiing; I allow the past to stay in the past and leave the future open. I recognize that abandoning my concepts may cause uncertainty, but I accept this small discomfort for the thrill of continually being surprised by ever-fresh experiences. The point of the discovery game is not to find out how good you are, but to experience your potential as it continues to reveal itself. Unlike many provers, the player of the discovery game

132

doesn't aim to ski beyond his potential; he is simply intent on breaking through the mental limits he has placed on it. He doesn't wish to be more than he is; he only wants to allow what is already there to manifest.

There is little more to be said about the discovery game, since each person has to decide in which areas he wishes to explore his potential, and then set out on that quest for himself.

Below are a few "unsticking" games that we've found useful to facilitate the transition from proving to improving.

Skiing as You Are

At the top of the slope, resist any inclination to try anything. Don't try to ski well or badly; don't try to relax or concentrate; don't try to let go. Simply trust and be aware. In fact, don't let any inner- or outer-game concept guide you; merely ski as you are and see what happens. It's very likely that if you let go of trying, your skiing will be better than usual, but don't form any conclusions about *how* it was better or what you must do to make sure it stays better. Don't attempt to ski the same way or improve on your first run. *Accept what happens.*

Continue this process until you feel you have given up making a conscious effort. The point of the game is to experience your skiing as it really is, without the "help" of Self 1.

Skiing Ignorant

A corollary of skiing as you are is a game whose only rule is to forget everything you think you know about skiing.

"How can I forget what I know?" demanded an irritated trial lawyer from New York.

"You can't," I replied, "but go ahead anyway. Erase as much as you can and see what happens. Don't think about how to make a turn, or whether you're doing it right."

"Wow! I don't believe it!" the lawyer said when he came to a stop at the bottom. "I skied just as well as when I was telling myself what to do."

"You looked better to me."

"I admit it was more enjoyable, but you can't expect me to believe that ignorance is the key to success."

"You were right the first time," I replied. "You can't forget what you know, but you can forget what you think you know—that is, concepts, images and beliefs. When you do, all that's left is what you *really* know. Maybe that's a more appropriate way of putting it: only know what you know."

Fun

Ski in such a way as to maximize the fun of the sport. Forget all the dos and don'ts and ski for pure enjoyment. Don't assume that the way you enjoy your first few runs is going to remain constant. Go beyond your concepts of what you *think* will be fun; focus on what is really fun for you. Give your body permission to behave in any way that it wants; let it play while you experience the pleasure of it. Increasing your speed may be fun, or perhaps decreasing it, or alternating the two—first a greater challenge, then a lesser one. Or focusing on fluidity and grace. Or being deliberately awkward or being aggressive may be fun for a while. Fun may even result from experimenting with how to increase your edge control.

After playing this game for a while, ask yourself whether the fun occurs more during the moments of action or after you or others have decided whether the action was good or bad. Does fun lie in the experience or in the afterthought?

Student Teacher

As stated before, most of us are unaware of the extent to which we limit ourselves by the roles we play. Last year I suggested to Julia, a high school student who was an early-intermediate skier struggling with doubts, that she pretend she was the instructor teaching the class how to make a stem turn. She blushed, stood stock-still for a moment, and then came out in front of the class. She began hesitantly, repeating what she'd heard about the rudiments of the turn, but soon seemed to lose herself in the role. She stopped trying to explain and demonstrated a couple of nearly picture-perferct turns. "That's how it should be done," she said coolly as we looked on amazed at the change in her skiing and self-assurance.

At first Julia was surprised, then almost embarrassed, by her new proficiency. "Gee, I never turned that well before," she said, and then, "How did you do that? That was a dirty trick."

"I didn't do it; you did. For a moment you became a part of yourself that can already do what another part of you says you can't. How did it feel to be the teacher?"

By perceiving the difference between our roles and who we really are, we can vastly extend the range of possibilities for ourselves.

Do It

Many skiers have had the experience of skiing behind an instructor and performing better than usual, often taking runs they never would attempt by themselves. It's not that the instructor has taught them something new, but that they trust him, and so Self 1, stops worrying and planning and giving instructions. Our abilities on these runs are an indication of how well we can ski when there is no Self 1 interference.

Recently I have been using this trust of the instructor in a more direct way. Last winter I was skiing with Diane, a nurse in her late twenties who had been on skis only three or four times. She was putting a lot of extra effort into her skiing, traversing from one side of the slope to the other, then making a 180-degree snowplow turn to traverse in the opposite direction. There wasn't much speed at the end of each traverse, so she had to push herself arduously through each turn. Knowing that she would have an easier time by following the fall line more closely, I yelled "Turn!" as she was halfway out of her first turn. She did so, and then another and another at my instruction. After five turns she stopped and said excitedly, "Wow! That was fun! I didn't think I could do that!"

"So how come you could?"

"Well, I trusted you. I knew that you wouldn't tell me to do something I couldn't, so I had no doubts."

"And I trusted you," I said. "I wouldn't have told you to turn if I hadn't know you could do it."

Diane's self-image had prevented her from having faith in herself. In trusting me, however, she actually was displaying some confidence in herself. Many skiers need the encouragement of an instructor or authority figure who believes in their potential more than they themselves do. But it is important that this trust be converted into self-trust by the student; otherwise he is left with the feeling that he can ski well only when the instructor is present. Such people don't seem to realize that it was *they* who skied the run, not the instructor.

Expressing Qualities

Identifying with Self 1 often causes us to focus on the existence of one quality or another in our self-image to the exclusion of others. For example, if I

137

consider myself cautious, I will not believe that I am adventurous. If I think that I am an aggressive skier, I probably won't see myself as one who allows the terrain to guide me. But the fact is that each of us has the capacity to express all qualities. We can be assertive and receptive, cautious and adventurous, calm and explosive. However, because we have stressed certain qualities in ourselves, these are more developed than others; they are giant oaks, while the others are still acorns. By believing that the acorn is not there—that we have no capacity for receptivity, for example—we tend to neglect it and to rely on what we are more familiar with. Thus any development of this quality is stunted.

The goal is not to stress one quality or another; it is to know that you are more than all of them combined, and to be able to choose which to express at different times. Achieving a harmony within all our qualities helps us to express who we are. The Chinese call it a balance of yin and yang—masculine and feminine, aggressive and receptive, hardness and softness. The person who recognizes and develops all his qualities can express each of them according to opportunities offered by different circumstances.

Is It All a Game?

Those who play the discovery game usually find that exploring the individual capabilities and talents of Self 2 is more enjoyable than the proving game of Self 1—and much more conducive to growth. But is it, too, just a game? What do we really win even if we succeed in skiing up to our potential? We win the enjoyment of the experience and the satisfaction of performing at our best, but is this enough to satisfy us? And if we don't succeed in skiing our best, have we really failed?

Earlier in this chapter, it was pointed out that the desire for improvement is natural, that man has a unique tendency to interfere with his own development, and that the primary means of interference is the forming of limiting images about himself, and of trying to prove his worth. Our universal tendency to create self-images has made me curious about why we do it. Why are we so eager to accept beliefs about who we are, to identify with our performance, appearance, and roles? Why is my self-image and the approval of others so important to me? Why do I need "self-respect" to prove to others that I am worthy of respect? Do other creatures have to prove their worth? Does a baby? Since I need to prove my worth only to the extent that I don't know it, I am left with only one possible answer to these questions. I don't know who I am! Not knowing, how can I know my value?

What is even more interesting is the realization that I must really want to know who I am. Why else would I spend so much time and energy trying to identify myself with so many superficial externals? Perhaps that's the beginning of the journey toward self-knowledge. I am he who wants to know who he is. I am distinct from the other organisms of the world in that not knowing who I am and where I'm going makes me uncomfortable. I thirst to know myself, but my thirst isn't quenched by ideas or images of who I am, no matter who agrees with them, but by experiencing that part of myself which is capable of satisfying my thirst. This experience goes beyond the scope of any game.

Learning New Skills

6

Few skiers want to spend more time than necessary learning something new. Having only a limited amount of time on the mountain, they sometimes become impatient when awareness techniques are used in an Inner Skiing lesson to help them develop a new skill. Often they feel that they are wasting their time if they are not getting a tip or technical correction, since this is the way they have been taught in the past and believe that it is the most direct route to immediate improvement.

The truth is that the more awareness you can bring to the practice of a new skill, the more easily, quickly and thoroughly you will learn it. Our experience with Inner Skiing has shown that by focusing attention on each step the body discovers the best way of executing it.

Peter

Peter, a shy thirteen-year-old, was an intermediate who had been skiing for three or four years and loved the sport. At the top of a run I suggested that we first take some warm-up turns.

I noticed that Peter stood stiffly on his skis and even sat back slightly as he went into a turn. As a result, his skis were moving out from under him and he didn't have enough edge control. He was also overweighting his uphill ski. The total picture was of a skier who lacked real control and balance, but who got by on his quickness and natural athletic ability.

"Let's take a short run, and you tell me where you feel your weight is," I suggested.

"I feel pretty far back when I'm turning," Peter said after about ten turns.

"Let's work on that, then. Sit as far back as your boots let you. Feel that?" He nodded. "Let's call that a three. Move a little further forward, but with your weight still mostly on your heels. Okay, that's a two. Now stand on the flat of your foot with your weight equally distributed. That's a one. Any time you're on the balls of your feet only, that will be a zero."

After Peter had practiced feeling the difference between these positions, we took a few more turns. "Notice where your weight is moment by moment," I told him, "and call out the numbers during the turn. Don't try to decide where it *should* be; just feel what is happening."

For ten more turns, Peter called out: "Three— two — three — four — Oops! — three — two — one —three—three—two—two—two—two. Gee," he said when we stopped, "I never realized how far back my weight was. I really felt off balance, as if I was always trying to catch up with my skis."

"Let's try it again. Remember, don't try to change what you're doing. Just notice it."

This time the first few numbers Peter called out were threes, but thereafter they were all ones or twos. He looked more on top of his skis and seemed to have more speed and control. "On those last few turns my weight was more on my whole foot. I felt more balanced, not so far behind," he observed.

"Good. This time I'd like you to do a couple of threes, then some twos, some ones, and even some zeros. Play back and forth between all the numbers."

After a dozen turns running through the numbers, we stopped and I asked Peter what he'd noticed. "It's hard to separate all the numbers, but one seemed to feel better than three. At zero I definitely felt that I could edge better, but it was a little scary, too."

I asked Peter to do the same exercise several more times without trying to decide what the "right" number was. "Just let your body do whatever it wants," I suggested.

Peter made a number of improved turns. His weight was forward more (mostly at one), his knees were in a deeper crouch and his entire stance was more relaxed, but his inside ski was overweighted during his turns.

At the top of the next run I said, "We're going to try something different. It's called Russian Skiing. It goes like this: notice when your weight is on both skis and when it is on one. When it's on both, yell out, 'Twoski, twoski,' and when it's on one, shout 'Oneski, oneski.' "

On Peter's first few turns, he was "twoskiing"; gradually, however, he started weighting the outside ski as he went into the turn. It was inspiring to see how quickly his body had picked up this fundamental skill.

Peter was laughing when he reached me. "That was fun," he said, and then told me how much better he felt and how much more control he had when he had "one-skiied."

"Do you remember which ski you weighted as you went into the turn?" I asked. Peter started to think about it, but I interrupted: "Let's find out. This time call out which ski your weight is on— right, left or both."

A few turns later Peter said, "I noticed that I'm almost completely on my outside ski as I go into the turn."

We practiced this awareness exercise until Peter was weighting his outside ski consistently.

Next I drew an S-curve in the snow diagraming a turn. I marked the top as 12:00, halfway through as 3:00 and the bottom as 6:00, then asked Peter to notice at what point he shifted his weight to his outside ski.

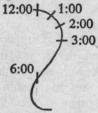

After ten or twelve turns, Peter told me that generally he stepped onto his outside ski at about 2:00.

"This time I'd like you to take some turns shifting your weight at twelve, and some at three. Notice what happens and how they feel."

We went all the way down the slope doing this exercise, and at the bottom Peter said, "Wow! I have much more control at twelve."

We took one last run, during which Peter turned beautifully. At the end of the lesson he looked up shyly and said, "I've never felt so good about learning. My father is a racing coach and he's good, but everything always seems so hard. I'm the youngest in the family, and I always seem to make mistakes. But today there were no corrections; I only had to concentrate on what was happening. No pressure, a lot of fun, and my skiing seemed to improve automatically. Thank you."

"Thank yourself," I said. "You did it, not me. You allowed your body to teach you what it wanted to. I was just there to help you focus your attention. Your body's pretty smart, and if you keep tuning into it you'll find that you can trust it to lead you in the right direction and that learning can always be fun."

Tips and Teachers

After watching Peter ski, it would have been easy to tell him what he was doing wrong and offer some suggestions. Seeing that he was sitting back, I could have told him to bend his knees more and to move his weight forward. But such instructions would probably have distracted his awareness of the immediate experience and actually hampered his improvement. Had he started thinking about instructions, repeating them in his mind and worrying about whether or not he was following them correctly, the sensory feedback he received from his body would have been less clear.

Tips fly around a ski slope like snowflakes in a blizzard: "Lean forward on ice," "Sit back on powder," "Roll your ankles into the turn," "Drive your knees into the hill," "Weight the outside ski" and so forth. But tips don't teach. Because they are concepts communicated by one Self 1 to another, they don't reach the skier's body. The body learns from its sensory experience and benefits from

147

conceptual instructions only as a guide to a given experience. From its performance it picks up data which are much more complex and refined than any that verbal instruction could possibly convey. The proper weight shift depends on such variables as the steepness of the slope, the length of the skis, and the skier's level of expertise. The calculations necessary to cover all these variables would be too numerous and complex to set down on paper, much less to memorize.

As Self 2 accumulates nonverbal data from its experience, it organizes the information it acquires in such a way that precise muscle instructions are generated and our responses become increasingly efficient and automatic. Once into the experience, the tip that got you there can be discarded. The map that guides you to a specific mountain in Vermont isn't needed once you're there. The map is not the territory; the concept is not the experience.

If you were to trace one of those skiing tips back to its origin, inevitably you would find that it started as someone else's experience. Someone skiing moguls discovered that pressing down on the tops of them achieved certain results. He passed this on to others, and eventually it filtered down to you and me. Too often we use the tip to replace the experience, rather than letting it guide us into it.

Constantly repeating technical instructions to yourself is an insult to Self 2, which can remember amazing complex body movements, whether or not they were ever conceptualized.

Helping Can Make You Helpless

Just as a skier can easily make his gospel a series of tips rather than his experience, he can also become overly dependent on his instructor. A teacher who likes to demonstrate how much more he knows than his student often reinforces the pupil's self-doubt. If the implication is that you cannot learn without the teacher's instructions, the student loses any reliance on his own natural learning process because he will be dependent on an outside authority for approval and guidance.

Learning happens best when both instructor and student recognize that experience is the teacher. The role of the instructor is to guide the student into experiences appropriate to his stage of development. At the same time that the student is guided toward attentive appreciation of the sensations of his body in relation to the snow and his skis, the instructor is learning from him how to best lead him to the next step. If the instructor is simply repeating a routine pattern tailored to, say, beginners, he will miss subtle clues about the student's immediate experience and will not be able to guide him effectively. Eager to take the student on to the next step, to get him through a progression in record time, he may not notice an uncertainty about the last step, or even that the student is experiencing fear or resistance. Only the instructor who trusts Self 2 can be of help in the learning process.

Breaking Habits

Often skiers reach a plateau at a certain point in their development. We can become stuck, for instance, somewhere between stem and parallel, and not seem to be able to get over that hurdle. We try everything—lessons, tips, instructional articles in ski magazines—but nothing seems to work.

Usually the cause of plateauing is an unconscious habit—a response to a certain situation which has become so ingrained that we no longer notice it. These habits can start when we are first learning to ski, but since they don't interfere with our initial progress, we remain unaware of them. Our bodies compensate for them, so that after a while they partially work. For example, a skier may be sitting back on her heels but be unaware of it because her body has compensated by shifting her trunk too far forward, doing double work to make up for the initial imbalance. When this posture has been held long enough, it comes to feel normal.

The key to breaking a habit is the same as for all natural learning: *increase your awareness.* In the darkness of unconsciousness habits persist—especially if we have prejudged them as bad, and blocked them so effectively that we don't even realize we have them. Hence, the first step in breaking a habit is to bring it into the light of your awareness. The second step is to do whatever you can to sharpen your focus on the specific characteristics of the habit. Only then does the necessary control emerge to change the pattern.

Since awareness of habits is usually suppressed, an instructor can be helpful in directing our attention to them. I am particularly conscious of this because of a recent confrontation with some of my own habits. I was a beautiful ballroom skier. My skis were always together and I had great form on all intermediate slopes, and even on some expert slopes. Still, when I came to a really tough run with a lot of moguls, I would start to lose my balance and timing. I would also feel tightness in my thighs after a few runs, no matter what slope I was skiing. Knowing that something was wrong, I tried various techniques and exercises in order to pinpoint the problem, but nothing seemed to help.

Then last winter at our Lake Eldora Clinic I took a lesson with Junior Bounouse from Snow Bird. After I had made about fifteen turns, he said, "Bob, this time I'd like you to spread your skis as far apart as you can and take ten turns that way." I did so, but it seemed strange. I felt about two feet shorter, like a mad midget. In order to turn in that direction, I had to lean over and weight my uphill ski much earlier. Nevertheless, as odd as this felt, I did notice that I seemed to have more control and balance even on difficult terrain.

Then Junior asked me to turn with my skis and legs as close together as possible. Since this was the way I usually skied, it felt more natural, but after a few minutes I noticed that something didn't seem right.

Junior asked me to switch back and forth several times between the two positions until we reached the bottom of the run. By then I had become aware of how forced my "ballroom" position was, and how much more tension there was in my thighs when my skis were kept together. Furthermore, my weight was often on the uphill ski as I came out of a difficult turn. As a result, my skis were sliding out from under me.

At the top of the next run, Junior said, "Now follow me without thinking about your legs or skis," and took off before I had a chance to respond. We tackled some pretty steep terrain with a lot of moguls, and I was amazed by my balance and control. After a few turns I began to notice that my skis weren't as close together as they'd been previously, and that I was stepping into my uphill ski earlier and more emphatically. My legs felt loose and relaxed, and responded fluidly to the terrain.

When I reported this to Junior as we came to a breathless stop, he said, trying to hide a grin, "C'mon, don't think about it. Let's go. You're wasting time." And he took off again.

It was a breakthrough run. I felt so balanced that I couldn't have fallen if I'd wanted to.

At another Inner Skiing clinic a few months later I joined a class led by Don Lemos from Aspen. Since my lesson with Junior my skiing had markedly improved, but I still felt that I was using too much effort, mostly in my upper body. After taking a run, Don said, "Bob, take a few turns as you normally do, but pay attention to how your head feels."

I did so, but was unaware of anything out of the ordinary. When Don asked what I'd felt, I replied, "Nothing," feeling silly and inspiring laughter from the rest of the class.

"Take a few more turns," Don persisted, "and see if you can tell whether your head is moving or if it's still."

My head felt just right—not too much movement, but not rigidly in place.

"Okay. Try a few more, but this time rock your head from side to side as much as you can whenever you turn."

This movement felt extremely awkward. Each time I rocked my head one way, I threw my body a little off balance, causing my skis to slide to the other side. But though it felt odd, I recognized something familiar in the motion. Then Don had me practice the other extreme—holding my head as still as possible during turns. I expected to feel stiff, but to my surprise I was much more balanced. We went through both variations a few more times, and soon I realized how much head rocking I had been doing before. At the end of the lesson when I took a run following Don's direction to forget everything I had just been doing, my body felt still and skiing became effortless.

Both Lemos and Bounouse had used the technique of exaggeration to help me become more aware of my habits, and this helped to bring them into clearer focus.

Being instructed to exaggerate a "bad" habit also tends to relieve it of any negative connotations, and therefore makes it more accessible to awareness. If a student is told that he isn't bending his knees enough at the end of a turn, the criticism usually produces a resistance to focusing attention on them: thinking that not bending is "bad," he tries to change the habit before really being aware of what he's doing. Not knowing how little his knees bend to begin with, the student finds change difficult. But if he is told to see what it feels like to ski without bending his knees at all, he soon

153

becomes aware of how ineffective this posture is, yet how similar to the way he had been holding himself, and he then begins to bend his knees by his own volition.

We all have habits. Some help us in reaching our goals, some don't matter, others are harmful. But any of them which are performed unconsciously detract from our overall sense of awareness of our lives. Unconscious habits put us to sleep and limit our alternatives; awareness awakens us to the range of our choices and potentials.

The Difficulty of Believing that Awareness Is Self-Corrective

"There's got to be more to it than that," a skier says, finding it hard to realize that awareness alone can bring about changes in his technique.

Even though I have seen awareness work wonders time and time again, the phenomenon still amazes me. Like most of us, I had always been conditioned to believe that improvement results from telling oneself what is wrong or right, and then trying hard to stop the one and do the other. This belief blocks us from trusting the natural learning that takes place if we are open to allowing it. Even skiers who have improved initially without a lot of instructions think that there must be a gimmick, and look for a tip to cling to as insurance. Often they give the power to the instructor, believing they can ski well only when he's around, but the fact is that improvement occurs whenever *awareness* is present. The evidence mounts: trying fails; awareness cures.

To dispel my own sense of disbelief I began wondering *how* awareness cures, and the following analogy came to mind. Suppose you are skiing late in the afternoon. There is a heavy snowfall, reducing visibility of the slope to about 10 percent. Assume also that you are skiing under the influence of a general anesthetic which cuts down the feeling of your body to 10 percent. With so little feedback from the terrain and from your body, it would be virtually impossible to get down the slope safely, much less improve your technique. The body needs visual and kinesthetic information to make even the simplest adjustment. As we become more aware, the feedback is increased, and the body's ability to correct itself increases proportionately.

Who Needs Practice?

Often the removal of a mental obstacle or an increase in awareness leads to significant and almost instantaneous improvements. Something new and dramatic emerges. Doing something well once or twice shows the skier his potential; he sees that the talent and skill are actually there, and, of course, he's excited. But if this leads him to believe that practice is unnecessary, he is liable to be disappointed the next day when his new skill has vanished. We can't consider ourselves improved until we can rely on our new-found ability being there when we need it.

Practice often sounds too much like drudgery to

someone brought up in a culture that believes in instant food, instant money, instant gratification. Everyone wants immediate results. We don't like to hear about how long it took to build Rome, or that enlightenment may take more than forty minutes a day. But the fact is that it takes time and practice to develop excellence in any endeavor. When a golfer or pitcher talks about "being in the groove," he is referring to a finely honed motion which took years to become ingrained. Just as cutting a groove in a piece of hard wood doesn't happen with one stroke, so learning to make a turn with ease on tricky terrain doesn't happen by doing it a few times. Self 2 needs repeated experience in order to refine its movements until an effective groove has been made.

But although I now realize that freedom and spontaneity come only from a lot of practice and self-discipline, I still believe in instant success. There is no reason why practice need be considered a form of torture which must be endured before the enjoyment of excellence is possible. Success can be had whenever awareness is fully present—at each step of the way, not just in reaching a final goal. It is because practice is so often regarded as something other than a truly experiential process that Self 1 gets bored so easily. After making twenty-five stem turns in a row, the mind tends to assume that it knows all about the maneuver; consequently we lose the attentiveness and curiosity which will make the twenty-sixth turn new and exciting. The succeeding turns are apt to be experienced through the dense fog of "Ho-hum, another stem turn." The ho-hum diminishes our receptivity; the bored mind skitters along the surface of the experience and is easily distracted because it doesn't perceive enough detail to hold its attention. When one is bored practicing, improvement is slow.

One way to overcome boredom is to learn to play. At a party I was introduced to a concert flutist, and eventually the talk turned to practice. "I never practice," he said. "I always play. I can play the scales for hours and have a marvelous time. I used to hate it when I was home practicing while everybody else was out having a good time. Then one day, instead of doing it by rote, I started experimenting with how hard I blew into the mouthpiece. I found that the sounds were different, depending on how hard or soft I blew, and this led me into listening to my breath as I played. I was delighted by all these subtle variations that I'd never heard before, and how I could control them. Now I can play scales every day for hours without being bored, and I never consider it practice any more."

One day I was teaching Ellen and Jean, sixteen-year-old twins from Texas who were very competitive with each other. They were full of enthusiasm and energy, always cutting each other off in mid-sentence. Intermediate skiers, they had just learned to step onto their outside ski to turn, but I felt they needed practice to groove their new skill.

When I took them to the top of an intermediate slope, Jean cried, "Hey, this is too easy! What a drag!"

"Yeah, let's hit an expert slope!" Ellen said.

It was easy to predict that the prospect of a half-hour's practice on weighting the outside ski would not be greeted by these two with much enthusiasm. Remembering my musician friend, I asked them to try something new. "If you don't like it, we'll take another run."

"We'll try anything once," they said warily.

"I want you to take a few turns and see if you can tell where in your body you feel the most pressure as you step on your outside ski in the turn. See how closely you can locate the exact spot."

Skiing down fifty yards, I stopped to watch. Rather than competing with each other or watching the teenage hotshots on the slope, their attention now seemed focused. When they reached me, they both started talking at once. "There was a lot of pressure right here above my right knee," Ellen began, but was interrupted by Jean. "First I felt my shin up against my boot, and then I started to feel the inside ball of my foot."

"All right. Let's see just how much pressure you have in these places," I said in an attempt to keep their interest level high. I explained the one-to-ten scale to them, and we took several runs, focusing on the parts of their bodies they had become aware of. While engrossed in these exercises, they were acquiring a lot of experience, and their weight shifts were becoming more refined.

At the top of the next run, Ellen said, "You know, I don't really like this numbers game much. It's too much like school. I have a better idea; let's call the scale rare, medium and burnt."

We tried this for a couple of turns. Not to be outdone, Jean then chimed in. "Let's try colors. Red will be a lot of pressure, white medium, and blue only a little."

After this, they started using code words, points, even boys' names on one run. I had no idea what they were talking about, but once in a while I would shift the focus of the drill to edge control or some other exercise, and they would invent a new way of playing with it.

After four or five long runs, the twins' skiing had improved noticeably, so I asked them if they wanted to try a more difficult run.

"No, we're having too much fun here," Ellen replied.

"We'll catch you after lunch," Jean called as they raced for the chair.

Challenging Yourself

Play is one of life's natural ways to avoid boredom. Challenge is another. Every skier has known the intense feeling of aliveness which comes when confronted with a trail slightly beyond his capabilities. This surge of sheer energy is our natural response to challenge; we "get up for it," as the saying goes, and often perform beyond our previous limits. Usually these peaks are reached when the challenge is not so far above our skill that fear or discouragement results, but is challenging enough to ensure attention. We can create appropriate challenges for ourselves during practice not only by attempting more difficult slopes, but also by reaching for higher levels of awareness and expertise. It can be just as satisfying to ski at relatively slow speeds tuning into the subtle body sensations—which indicate, for example, small but significant differences in degree of edging—as it is to race full speed through a mogul field.

Practice off the Slopes: Skiing in Your Mind's Eye

An increasing number of professional and world-class athletes are using a mental skill called visualization to heighten concentration, refine skills and prepare themselves for competition. It is said that before each game Jimmy Brown, the legendary all-pro fullback for the Cleveland Browns, used his imagination to picture each play in which he would be involved and how he would react in it. Jean-Claude Killy and many other skiers have also used visualization the night before a race. Killy told a friend of mine that one night when he was practicing this he saw himself fall at one gate. Running through the inner movie again, he fell at the same gate. This time, however, he noticed that his line into the gate had been too extreme and so he had caught an edge. In his mind's eye he was able to correct the line and ski the gate perfectly. Taking the same line the next day, he won the race.

There is nothing mystical about visualization. It is simply the use of imagination and memory as a mental exercise. It is one way of practicing the best of the images that Self 2 has in its memory bank, thereby forming effective grooves. When visualizing a movement, it is most effective to see the image in as much detail as possible, and also to feel it kinesthetically. Experience what you would be feeling if you were actually skiing: your weight shifting as you make a turn, the wind in your face,

160

your various muscles working. Hear the sound of your skis on the snow. Make your images as graphic as possible. When skiing is rehearsed in this way, many of the benefits of actual practice are approximated. Studies on visualization have shown that when a person sees in his mind's eye a physical activity, small but measurable amounts of contraction take place in the muscles associated with the maneuver, and that the same neurological pathways are excited by an imagined movement as by an actual one.

However, visualization cannot be a substitute for actual practice. It is only a supplement whose effectiveness depends on the depth of your awareness and ability to concentrate.

A Skill Worth Practicing

Practice requires motivation, and motivation requires recognition of the importance of the practice. Nobody will try to perfect a parallel turn unless skiing is important to him. Instead of regarding practice as the repetition of various physical exercises, the Inner Skier recognizes that he is also exercising important inner skills. Primarily he is disciplining the focus of his awareness or concentration. Some skiers use concentration to improve, but the Inner Skier places its value above the benefits it brings to his technique on the mountain. He recognizes that improvement in skiing will be useful only on the slopes, whereas concentration is a skill that is desirable in every human activity. For the Inner Skier it makes more sense to ski in order to increase his concentration than to concentrate in order to improve his skiing. Developing the art of concentration is probably the most practical and universally beneficial skill a human being can develop; it is the subject of the next chapter.

7

Relaxed Concentration: The Master Skill

Throughout my youth it seems I was always being told to pay attention and not let my mind wander. This advice from coaches, teachers and parents usually came when I was performing poorly. If I struck out, there was that familiar reminder to keep my eye on the ball; if I didn't know the answer in class, I was told to stop dreaming. I would try hard to pay attention, but somehow fantasizing about the girl with long braids in the third row or being a famous baseball star seemed more interesting than learning the capital of Ecuador or the square root of 625.

Inevitably I would be sent down to the principal's office: "Young man, you've got to learn to concentrate or you'll never amount to anything!" But since I hadn't yet reached my teens, getting ahead in the world wasn't as important as playing in the park with my friends, so I didn't pay attention to him either.

Still, the message that concentration was necessary if I wanted to perform well did filter through my resistance. When I am having a bad run skiing, for instance, I am aware that it is usually because my mind is not focused on what I am doing. I know that if I don't pay attention I'm going to have a disastrous day, so I tell myself that I have to concentrate. After a while this becomes "Concentrate, damn it!" But this attempt to force concentration results in a wrinkled brow, clenched jaw, tight shoulders and arms. At this stage, focusing attention is difficult because I am concentrating on *trying to concentrate* rather than on my skiing. As a result, I don't feel my body or skis or see the slopes clearly; I have substituted one set of distractions for another, as well as increasing tension and tightness.

What Is Concentration?

When concentration is painful, difficult or strained, it is no longer concentration. Notice the absorption of children at play and you will see a beautiful example of what concentration is. The child's mind is relaxed but totally engaged. There is no thinking about the activity—just pure experiencing. The attention of the child is focused on everything he's doing, and though it may not stay long on a single object, it passes from one interest to another in an unbroken flow. Or watch a cat waiting in the grass for a gopher to emerge. Its attention is held steadily for long periods of time, its body poised, waiting for the moment of action. To remain steadily focused, does the cat have to tell itself, "I gotta concentrate, I gotta concentrate"? We can learn the simple lesson of relaxed concentration from small children and animals just as we did the natural learning process.

Human beings concentrate best when they're not trying hard to do so, but are simply interested in what's taking place. During an exciting movie the audience doesn't have to remind itself to watch the screen.

The simple law of concentration is that it follows interest. Where our interest is, our mind is. If the interest is strong, concentration will follow. If the interest is weak, attention will be easily distracted. We have to force concentration only when we are trying to focus on something we really are not interested in at that moment. When a person is somewhere he doesn't want to be, he does so in body only and lets his mind escape. We've all had the experience of talking to a person who is really a million miles away, even as he smiles and nods appropriately. Indeed, we have all been that person from time to time; we allot 10 percent of our attention to present circumstances; the other 90 percent is somewhere else.

The ability of the mind to flee the present is another unique capability of the human species. Or perhaps it is the same capability we use to interfere with our learning and growth. Babies and animals don't become lost in mind trips into the not-here and not-now. But the adult mind can all too easily escape the present reality and in an instant be anywhere else in the universe.

Earlier we compared awareness to light. Paying attention means focusing the light of awareness in order to see further, deeper or in greater detail in a particular direction. To pursue this analogy, concentration is similar to turning a 1000-watt bulb shining equally in all directions into a beam of light that focuses on a target. When the diffused light becomes a beam, we no longer see the surroundings, but we greatly increase our awareness in the single direction the ray is shining. Concentration is simply the process of focusing the light of attention, of turning the beam into a laser-like ray.

When we lose attentiveness, the light energy of our awareness is diffused. We may have 1000 watts to illuminate what is happening to our bodies and skis on the snow, but if part of our awareness is wasted in thinking about such future possibilities as how well we're going to ski this run, whether we might be hurt or the like, and another part is remembering past mistakes, and still a third part is thinking about business or how things are back home, we will have very little awareness to devote to our skiing. In such circumstances it's easy to miss details of the terrain or the messages your body is sending you.

The Importance of Concentration

Every Inner Skiing exercise mentioned in this book so far has been a practical application of the simple principle of relaxed concentration. But though the importance of a concentrated mind to achieve high levels of performance is well recognized, the need for it in the learning process is not sufficiently acknowledged. Learning is a simple function of memory. If Self 2 didn't automatically remember its skiing experiences, every run would be like your first. The images in Self 2's memory bank are essential to good skiing. What is in the memory bank of an expert skier? First, it obviously is packed with images, primarily visual and kinesthetic impressions. But good skiing is not simply the result of the *quantity* of images in the bank; their *quality* is what counts most. For example, if the skier is scared most of the time, the images he retains are going to be out of focus and therefore less useful. Likewise, if he is bored, and goes through repetitious movements without interest, he may accumulate a lot of dull images which lack enough vividness to stand out in sharp contrast. Skiing scared is like shaking the camera; skiing bored is like taking a picture without enough light. Neither produces the necessary clarity of image. On the other hand, if the camera is still and there is enough light on the scene, a clear picture will be stored from which Self 2 can extract accurate muscle instructions for the future. Self 2 can learn more from clear images of mistakes than from blurred, dull images of a good run. Excellent skiing results from a large number of high-quality images.

The enjoyment inherent in concentration also needs to be stressed. As a person can concentrate, so he can enjoy. Whenever we let our minds become truly absorbed in an activity, it is enjoyable. Even the most simple and unchallenging actions become a pleasure to perform when our attention is wholly present. Perhaps that's why children laugh so easily. When the mind is absorbed, it is quiet and doesn't want to wander. When restlessness disappears, we enjoy; conversely, when our minds are inattentive, we experience discomfort.

Who Is in Control of Your Attention?

Who or what chooses where our attention goes? Can you consciously decide to keep your attention on the present moment—on skiing, for instance—and have your mind happily obey? Or does it seem to have a will of its own? Often our attention seems to be a slave to the whim of the frequent and conflicting desires of Self 1. Who can order his mind to stop thinking and focus on the experience? Will your mind keep focused on the tennis ball, or the edges of your skis, or on this problem, or this book, for as long as you ask it to? Any of us can make such a request, but we seldom do, because we know that our minds probably won't obey, and then we would be confronted with the unpleasant fact that our attention is not under our control.

The practice of relaxed concentration is an attempt to regain a fundamental human freedom: the freedom to experience whatever in life we consider most satisfying, beautiful and true. When we practice keeping our attention focused on the goal of our choice we begin to regain that freedom and the power that comes with it. To the extent that a person loses his ability to concentrate, he himself becomes powerless to accomplish, to enjoy and, above all, to love.

We love that which we give our concentration to, and we concentrate on that which we love. The person who has a passion for skiing will have no difficulty concentrating, practicing and performing, but the individual who is on the mountain primarily for some other reasron—for example, to prove something to himself or others—is more in love with his image than with skiing and is apt to find himself easily distracted.

Choosing to Concentrate

Concentration is a discipline we impose on ourselves for a purpose, We are used to constraining our bodies; for instance, we give up a large measure of physical freedom for five to six hours when we fly from New York to Los Angeles, but in doing so we reach our destination quickly. Likewise, when we choose to concentrate, we sacrifice the freedom of our minds to take excursions into the past or future. When we choose to go skiing in the first place, we are forsaking a book, business or the Caribbean for the sake of what we hope to experience by skiing. Every act of saying yes to one activity requires saying no to many others. To deliberately make the choice of a particular person or activity is therefore a profound compliment. On the other hand, to be involved only in terms of physical presence is an insult not only to that person or activity but also to yourself,

Once the decision to go skiing has been made and you are standing at the top of the slope, there are still numerous choices. If you want most to improve your form, it might be best to focus attention on your body and listen to its kinesthetic feedback. Increasing concentration in order to overcome fear is another alternative. Or if you are interested in simply having fun and letting yourself go, you may decide to try to abandon all Self 1 control and let your run take you for a ride. There are innumerable choices; all that is important is to make one of them. Otherwise Self 1 will have a hundred ideas for you simultaneously: I've got to perfect this turn before the end of the day . . . I should be practicing my pole plants . . . I wonder if there's anyone to ski with this run . . . I should be concentrating more . . . I should be relaxing more . . . The instructor said I wasn't rolling my knees enough to the inside . . . Maybe I'm thinking too much. Without choosing to concentrate, Self 1 can drive you crazy with inner- and outer-game thoughts, scattering your energy in many directions.

Making the choice to concentrate is to practice disciplining your mind and directing your own awareness. It isn't necessary to stay on a single object of concentration for an entire day, but it is a good idea to focus on a single target for a reasonable period—at least until it is no longer producing benefits or retaining your interest. The discipline of sustained focus is an important part of the process of concentration, but extending it is possible only if you don't force it.

For instance, if you decide to try to increase awareness of your edges for two or three runs, and your mind starts thinking about bending your knees or about your ride up in the chair lift or anything else, don't be angry at yourself; simply bring your concentration back gently. Training the mind is like teaching a wild animal; if you punish it for not obeying you, it will turn on you. Firm but gentle persuasion works better. With continued practice the mind increasingly comes under our control. The process is slow and gradual, but constantly rewarding. The ultimate goal is freedom from mind's wayward desires, freedom to employ it as a servant rather than to be its slave.

Practices in the Art of Relaxed Concentration

Parking the Mind

When a person decides he wants to begin the practice of controlling his mind, what is most important to remember is that true concentration is a relaxed state of mind. Take the example of a skier who after a couple of "bad" runs recognizes that it is his lack of concentration which is keeping him from performing at his best. He decides he must concentrate more and tries to force it, but his skiing only becomes worse and he soon finds himself tense and frustrated. Finally he gives up and says, "The hell with this, I'm just going to have some fun." He takes off down the slope whistling a tune, forgetting all his problems, and has a marvelous run. He concludes that he skis much better when he's not concentrating.

Although many of us have drawn this same conclusion in similar situations, it is not that we ski better when we aren't concentrating but that we concentrate better when we're not trying to. With the song in his head the skier was occupying his striving mind, reducing his tension and freeing Self 2.

Many people unconsciously tend to sing or hum to themselves to relax their minds and induce a corresponding rhythm in the body. Last year in an Inner Skiing class, Carl Wilgus from Sun Valley asked us to sing a song as we took a run. For some reason I chose "Tea for Two," and I skied down the fall line just as if I were dancing to this old melody. At "tea" my skis would turn to one side, and at "two" they would have already shifted to the other. I wasn't thinking about what I was doing; I was skiing as if I had nothing to do with what was happening. It was a wonderful run; I moved better and more gracefully than ever before. When I stopped and watched the others in the class, I felt that I knew the rhythm of the song each was singing by the way they were skiing. Carl, who had "boogied" down the slope, had been singing the Beatles' "Eight Days a Week." Another, who seemed almost in a trance, had been humming "Moon River." Everyone enjoyed the exercise so much that we traded songs and danced the rest of the way down.

This stage of concentration, which could be called "parking the mind to music," is like counting sheep to help us fall asleep. The exercise distracts our mind and lulls it into a rhythm which induces sleep. As the mind relaxes, the anxious thoughts that were keeping us awake or interfering with our skiing disappear.

There are many ways besides music to involve Self 1 harmlessly while simultaneously evoking qualities helpful to our skiing. For instance, imagining yourself as an animal can be both effective and fun. In one class we created a zoo. I chose to be a lion; other students selected a snake, a leopard, a gazelle, an eagle and even a chipmunk. We came down the mountain roaring, hissing and squeaking, and each person's skiing actually resembled the animal he had chosen. I was aggressive, the leopard was graceful, the gazelle was elegant, the snake slithered and the eagle floated—but

I never could figure out what the chipmunk did.

Many people are under the impression that you have to be serious to focus the mind, but having fun is actually conducive to concentration. When the mind is enjoying itself it is not so easily distracted.

In another exercise I sometimes choose a word conveying a specific quality I want to evoke on my next run. Repeating a word such as "aggressive," "graceful," "easy" or "smooth," my body tends to reflect that quality in its movements. Again, the trick is to absorb Self 1 in the rhythm and meaning of words so that your true potential will be freed. The music or evocative symbol shouldn't be one that requires much conscious effort; the purpose of the exercise is simply to occupy Self 1's attention while the greater part of our awareness automatically attends to our skin.

Direct Concentration

There are two basic functions of any practice of concentration. One is to decrease the interference of Self 1; the other is to increase our awareness. Parking the mind occupies Self 1, but it doesn't necessarily increase feedback. Both goals can be accomplished simultaneously by focusing on something that is happening and is directly pertinent to our skiing. Think of everything that is involved when you ski: body, terrain, sounds, knees, shins, arms, ankles, skis, edges, snow. Anything you can sense, feel, see or hear when skiing is an appropriate object for concentration.

Foot Concentration

One of the most vital yet most overlooked areas of concentration when you are skiing is your feet. They are connected to your skis and they affect every movement you make. "A good racer's concentration," writes Warren Witherell in *How the Racers Ski*, "is on the feel of his edges in the snow. He can feel the texture of the snow, the shape of the terrain, and he is sensitive to the flex and shape of his skis."

Boone Lennon, an instructor and racing coach at Sun Valley, once told me that he seems to feel every inch of his skis when he is going down a mountain: "It is as if my skis were part of me." In order to develop sensitivity of this sort, it is necessary to heighten the awareness of your feet, to sense each part of them in detail. The next time you ski, focus on the soles of your feet. Feel how the weight is distributed: is it more on the balls of your feet, the heels, the insides or the outsides? Notice where your weight is when you traverse, and how the pressure shifts during a turn. To keep your mind involved, call out where this pressure is at different times during a run and rate it on a numbered scale. This kind of detail can keep your mind absorbed, which makes you more sensitive to your body's feedback. One caution: don't become overly concerned about the accuracy of your numbers—call them out quickly without thinking.

After a while, awareness of your feet will extend to your skis and you will be able to feel their flex, the subtle changes in terrain, and the bite of your edges on the snow. Can you imagine how well you could ski if you had the awareness and control of your skis that you have of your feet? Or better yet, if you had the control of your feet and skis that you have of your hands? Think of how subtle and fine your turns would be with this degree of awareness.

Foot awareness can also be practiced off the mountain by noticing how your foot lands and where the most pressure is when walking or running. Many skiers lose this awareness when their boots are too tight or their feet are cold. They curl their feet, which is not only uncomfortable and cuts off feeling, but also causes tension in the ankles, shins and calves, preventing flexibility and fluidity of movement. Cramped toes make it painful to put our weight forward, and usually cause us to lean back, a dangerous habit which can cause a lot more pain than in our toes. A good way to experience foot awareness is to try the following exercise. Take your shoes off and place your right foot on a tennis ball. Let the ball roll under the foot, feel it make firm contact with every part of it. Then stand on both feet and note how your right foot feels in comparison with the other. Most people find that it will be more relaxed, more in contact with the floor and more sensitive.

Skiing Centered

When Self 1 is in control, our attention is usually in our heads. When we think too much, we tend to become top-heavy, as if there were extra weight above our shoulders, and consequently we easily lose balance. But when we move freely and easily in a state of relaxed concentration, our natural center of gravity—the point of perfect balance—is located just below the navel. If you watch great athletes or dancers closely, you will see that their movements seem to originate from this center.

Last year I gave a class three technical instructions at once and asked that everyone do his best to follow them. Trying to implement them on the next run made each student think a lot, thus keeping the focus fully centered in his head. The next time we came down the mountain I suggested that everybody shift his attention to his pelvis. Afterwards the response from the class was unanimous. When the focus was centered in the mind, the students couldn't feel their feet or skis, and their heads hung forward as if leading their bodies. Everyone felt off balance, awkward and mechanical. However, when their attention was on their natural center, they reported that they felt more relaxed in the upper part of their bodies and that their skiing felt smooth, flowing, balanced and effortless. Centering also results in greater stability and gives the skier better contact with the snow, which in turn leads to better control.

Peter Bissett, an instructor from Lake Eldora, recommends that students imagine they are skiing at night with a flashlight in their bellies which shines on the terrain in front of them, showing them where to go. This simple exercise focuses concentration and encourages the initiation of movements from the skier's center of balance rather than from his head or shoulders.

Seeing

Though excellence in skiing is mainly dependent on the quality of kinesthetic feedback, visual feedback is also essential. The eyes act like a scanner, constantly giving us input regarding subtle changes in the pitch of the slope and the texture and depth of the snow. The body will react to what the eyes see as long as Self 1 doesn't screen off this information by making judgments.

One way of increasing visual concentration is to pretend that the ski slope is a giant canvas and that your skis are brushes. Each run you take becomes a stroke on the painting and each turn a curve. Looking down the slope before and while skiing it, you can imagine what kind of stroke would be best on this particular terrain—long, short, smooth or squiggly. Your eyes then guide your body through your run; you simply let the changes in terrain teach you how to "paint" them. Since we see better when we don't think that we know everything about a trail, it's a good idea when practicing visual concentration to ski it as if for the first time.

The next time you ski, notice how far ahead of the tips of your skis your eyes fall naturally. Many people, concerned with the position of their skis, tend to look at them constantly, and thus don't gain feedback from the slope. Others look too far ahead. Experiment with focusing on different distances until you settle on what works best for you.

Listening to Your Skis

Most skiers will concentrate either on the feelings of their bodies or on seeing the trail; it rarely occurs to them to listen to the sound of their skis. But if you listen closely you can hear distinct variations when the skis are flat or on edge. Even the varying conditions of the snow create different sounds. By involving the additional sense, that of hearing, our minds become even more concentrated, and the feedback we receive increases our control.

One day, while listening to my skis as I practiced, I began carving beautiful turns with virtually no skidding. There was a smooth and muffled sound, as opposed to the *whoosh* of a skid. Resisting the temptation to analyze what I was doing right, I simply asked my body to keep reproducing the sound. It worked; holding the sound in my mind, to my amazement my body kept reproducing it. Occupying Self 1 with the memory of the sound of a carved turn, Self 2 was free to repeat the actions which had produced the sound.

Broad and Narrow Concentration

The choice of what to concentrate on is easy if you want to practice edge control or if your pole plant is so rough that it throws your timing off. That is, you focus on something that is relevant to those difficulties. However, occasionally there is nothing specific that you want to concentrate on; no single problem seems more important than another. At such times simply keep your awareness general; instead of narrowing your field of concentration, broaden it.

If concentration is like a light shining upon a target, general concentration would resemble a broad searchlight. A wide focus on your body will reveal any tension or imbalance which needs particular attention. When such a problem emerges, you can turn your broad searchlight into a more powerful and focused beam to acquire more feedback from that area.

If you focus for too long on one area of your body or your skiing, concentration might become strained, and it is then time to relax and return to a more general awareness. Broaden your light again and become aware of your rhythm or balance as you come down the mountain. Sooner or later something more specific will again emerge. It is perfectly natural for your concentration to veer between the general and the specific as you ski.

Breaking Through Your Mind

In the stages of concentration discussed so far, the mind has been either "parked" or focused, but in the breakthrough stage of concentration your busy, chattering mind stops altogether and you enter into a world that is pure experience. You are calm, quiet, immersed in your activity. There is no separation between action and awareness, thinking and doing. You are in total harmony with yourself and your surroundings, and all else—time, space, past and future—pales before the present moment. Athletes call this state "playing unconscious," or being "out of your head."

Fine, says Self 1, but how do you get yourself into this state? Ay, there's the rub; you can't make it happen any more than you can make yourself fall asleep. You can prepare yourself for sleep by lying down on a comfortable bed, closing your eyes and relaxing your mind, but the final stage can't be forced. Similarly, you can't control the attainment of the state of oneness, but you can prepare for it so that it is more likely to happen. In the final analysis, the breakthrough stage of concentration is a process of letting go, so don't look forward to congratulating yourself if you do achieve it, because the instant you do so you've returned to your thinking mind.

The Master Skill

Whatever experience we gain in the practice of relaxed concentration helps us understand the theory behind it; conversely, as our understanding of the theoretical aspects develops, our practice improves. Theory without practice won't help us, but the necessary practice won't occur unless we understand the importance of concentration in our lives.

Earlier it was stated that concentration is a voluntary discipline that we impose on our minds for a purpose. If the reader's primary goal is to improve his skiing, then his practice will be only as diligent as the importance he places on the sport. But relaxed concentration, though necessary to excellence in skiing, is also a requisite for any kind of excellence. The very quality of our daily experience depends on the development of this master skill. The quality of our concentration can make the difference between a life that is satisfying and alive and one that is incomplete and dull.

Two skiers can stand atop the same mountain, and one can be experiencing a transcendent beauty while the other is seeing just another mountain. The difference in the quality of their perceptions lies in the quality of their attention. Similarly, you can ski a beautiful run but not really appreciate it, while on another day you can take the same run with less proficiency but, because of the quality of your concentration, really enjoy yourself and learn more from the experience. Skiing well doesn't automatically lead to experience that is good, nor does skiing poorly have to lead to one that is bad. What makes the difference is the ability of the skier to appreciate whatever happens.

This understanding is really the essence of Inner Skiing. The quality of our enjoyment and the excellence of our performance depend primarily on *internal* conditions. Value lies *within*, not without. A small improvement in our internal ability to perceive can outweigh many external changes because it has the power to change the entire range of one's experience.

Take an example. If you take home movies with a motion-picture camera that has a scratched lens and a faulty shutter, what success will you have? The footage shot with such a camera is going to be inferior, but you might mistakenly conclude that it was the locale you chose. Of course, the film still doesn't come out well, whatever spot you pick, so you may end up complaining that there's no place on earth that will give you the footage you want. However, if the scratches are removed and the shutter repaired, it will make all the difference in giving you a successful film of even an ordinary place.

This camera analogy does not fit our human situation in one important way: that is, a camera is not affected by the object it is exposed to, but a human being is. A person who enjoys fine music will be uplifted by it, and his ability to appreciate it will be increased by its quality. Likewise, a steady diet of inferior music tends to lower the consciousness of the experience and make it more difficult, if not impossible, for him to value an especially fine piece of music.

Hence, it is common sense to seek out those experiences that are conducive to uplifting our awareness, not only because the experience itself will be more satisfying, but because it prepares us to better appreciate the next one. What good will it do a man to be in an ideal situation if, because of an uncontrolled mind, he is not aware enough to appreciate it?

My father used to tell me the story of a guard at the Louvre whose job was to protect the "Mona Lisa." Often tourists would come up with cameras, stare at the painting and turn to him and say, "What's so beautiful about her?" His reply was always the same: "Monsieur (or madame), it is not this picture which is on trial."

Skiers and nonskiers alike tend to assume that the quality of their experience is the result of what is happening to them, so we put too much energy into changing externals. We look for better ski tips, better jobs, better homes, better husbands and wives. Although we can alter our lives by changing our environment, most significant changes occur when we find effective ways to change our inner landscape, because that is the environment that we will always have with us.

Experiencing is our fundamental activity, and so the quality of our lives depends on the quality of our experience. And the quality of experience depends on state of mind and on depth of concentration. If my life isn't as satisfying as it could be, is this the fault of my circumstances or of my ability to appreciate them? Is the cause of my discontent internal or external? Are not most of our external conflicts a result of our internal unrest? Must of the time we are so caught up in the content of our lives, the "goodness" or "badness" of what happens to us, that we forget to take any joy in the very fact that we are alive and are able to experience life at all. Regardless of the texture of our lives, we are privileged to be participating in the process called living. Whenever I can see my life from this point of view, I begin to free myself of the pettiness of Self 1 concerns, and to appreciate the best my life has to offer. And with what do I appreciate it? With the gift of awareness, with the quality of my attention and with the power of my concentration.

Beyond Inner Skiing

by Timothy Gallwey

Though we have suggested throughout this book that Inner Skiing presents opportunities to improve not only your skiing but also the quality of your life, it should be made clear, before ending, that the benefits of the sport are limited. No matter how much we learn about relaxed concentration or how beautiful our breakthrough experiences, skiing can give us only fleeting glimpses and indirect hints of the breakthroughs we can hope to experience on a more lasting basis. Yet the breakthroughs we do attain on the mountain indicate that there are levels of awareness possible for us which are more beautiful and deeply satisfying than we ordinarily reach in our everyday lives.

But how long can skiing keep one in this wonderful state? Even if we had a breakthrough every time we skied, the moment would always arrive when we'd have to take our final run, pack up our skis and return to our daily life. What will keep the freshness of our experience from fading into the routine of our usual patterns of thought and behavior? How do we recapture the same clarity of awareness without the exhilaration of skiing to quiet our minds?

For those readers interested in seeking ways to a more permanent breakthrough experience beyond the interference of Self 1—or what amounts to the same thing, to answer the basic question of human identity raised in Chapter 5—it would not seem right to leave the impression that either skiing or the principles of Inner Skiing per se could give them complete satisfaction.

The hope for a continuing breakthrough cannot be fulfilled on the slopes, on the tennis courts or anywhere else for that matter, except deep within one's self. Yet it would also seem wrong to complete this book without expressing the recognition that it is possible to move beyond the limitations of Self 1. We can, through growth, guidance and experience, achieve a lasting state of consciousness that none of us would want to trade for a lifetime of skiing breakthroughs. The breakthroughs on the slopes are only intermittent indications of far greater experiences attainable by skiing the "inner slopes."

Inside all of us is a mountain with no top and no bottom. The skiing there is perfect. The snow is made of pure peace and there is not a trace of Self 1 interference. The chair lift is always available and takes a person as high as he wants to go. Skiing this inner mountain has the power to satisfy the human longing to know oneself and the reason for which one was born. This place of perfect peace has always been within us waiting to be sought, but it can be enjoyed only by those who have recognized the limitations of seeking this satisfaction externally.

This mountain is our true self. Skiing it with steady concentration erodes the power of Self 1 to trick us into thinking that we are separate and alone. It leads us to the source of the love and peace which all of us seek. Beyond the barriers of Self 1, inner and outer merge and it becomes possible to live in a changing world while being fully aware of that core which does not change.

I would not hold out this possibility of self-knowledge for readers if it were not a matter of my own personal experience and if I did not believe it worth every sincere effort to find. To aim for less is to fall short of realizing the most important potential each of us possesses.

ABOUT THE AUTHORS

TIMOTHY GALLWEY, once a nationally ranked junior tennis player, was captain of the Harvard tennis team in 1960. Interested in principles of learning, he helped establish an innovative liberal arts college in the Midwest. Thereafter his desire for more profound answers led him on a world-wide search, which culminated in a deep commitment to an inner search through the technique of meditation as taught by Guru Maharaj Ji. From the process of quieting his own mind came the insights into learning and performing which resulted in two currently successful books, *The Inner Game of Tennis* and *Inner Tennis*. Of the many who saw the broad applications of Inner Game principles, skiers were among the most enthusiastic: hence *Inner Skiing*. Mr. Gallwey now lives in Los Angeles, lecturing, training professionals and working on future Inner Game books.

BOB KRIEGEL is a humanistic psychologist whose area of specialization is self-realization through sports and games. A high school All-American swimmer, captain of his college lacrosse team and a skier for over twenty years, Mr. Kriegel has been involved with the mental aspects of sport since the early seventies when he helped found the Esalen Sports Center. He was also the director of SAGAS, a training project for professional educators and psychologists in the use of sports for self-development. In addition to conducting *Inner Skiing* programs for ski instructors and the public, he has lectured throughout the country on new approaches to sport and self-understanding. Currently he and his family live in San Francisco.

IF YOU LIKED THIS BOOK

YOU'LL LOVE THE INNER SKIING EXPERIENCE

we invite you to

SKI OUT OF YOUR MIND

with us

for information on Inner Skiing programs at some of the worlds finest resorts, send the coupon below:

INNER SKIING
10 Encline Ct.
San Francisco, CA 94127

NAME

ADDRESS

CITY

STATE/ZIP